Studies in
EPHESIANS

Studies in
EPHESIANS

by

W. Leon Tucker

KREGEL PUBLICATIONS
Grand Rapids, Michigan 49501

Studies in Ephesians by W. Leon Tucker.
Copyright © 1983 by Kregel Publications,
a division of Kregel, Inc. All rights reserved.

Library of Congress Cataloging in Publication Data

Tucker, W. Leon (Walter Leon), 1871-1934.
  Studies in Ephesians.

  Reprint. Originally published: "With Him," or,
Studies in the Epistle to the Ephesians. New York :
Book Stall, 1917.
  1. Bible. N.T. Ephesians — Criticism, inter-
pretation, etc. I. Title.
BS2695.T8   1983   227'.506   83-6115
ISBN 0-8254-3828-4 (pbk.)

Printed in the United States of America

DEDICATED TO
PAUL RADER
A friend, in the fellowship of the
faith, and a beloved brother in the
bond of the Body of Christ.

CONTENTS

8 *CONTENTS*

**Part 1
Introduction
Ephesians 1:1-2**

1

INTRODUCTION

FREE FROM ALL apologetics of human reason and speech, the Word of God in its opening statement authoritatively declares: "In the beginning God created the heavens and the earth." Thus we are introduced to the Creator and His creation and are instructed concerning the scope and the twofold sphere of this creation, namely, "the heavens and the earth" (R.V.). These two spheres are again brought before us in later Scriptures, the Epistles of Paul (Colossians, Philippians), where we see them related not only to the creation but to redemption. Things concerning the first-mentioned sphere, "the heavens," is not the subject of the Bible, for the major portion of the Bible is concerning the "earth," not the "heavenlies." Credit has been given a great astronomer for a pertinent remark that "the Bible was not written to tell how the heavens go, but to tell how to go to heaven."

Whatever truth this statement may include, it is quite sure the Bible, in the body of its writings, is not concerned with affairs in the heavens, but rather with events related to the earth. Sir Robert Anderson, in his *The Coming Prince,** says:

> The Bible is far more than a textbook of theology and morals, or even than a guide to heaven. It is a record of the progressive revelation God has vouchsafed to man and the Divine history of our race in connection with that revelation.

*Sir Robert Anderson, *The Coming Prince* (Grand Rapids: Kregel Publications, 1957), pp. 14-15.

From the first and faithful record of the original creation (Gen. 1:1) to the recreation and restoration of the original creation (Gen. 1:1 to 2:1), and forward on to the consummation recorded in the Book of Revelation, the Scriptures hold constantly before us the one great and principal truth that God has chosen the earth on which to enact an earthly program, with an earthly people, the same issuing in earthly blessing. The world that now is, took order and organization to become the home of man, who is created in the image of God, and who at the proper time is placed in dominion over it (Gen. 1:26, 28). Its fullness and fruit is at his disposal and its plentitude placed at his hand (Gen. 1:29, 31).

Man has come for a long tenure, and the successive seasons, occurring, concurring and recurring, are guaranteed and assured by God in the terms of the lease granting man possession for a period of great extent.

When sin enters the world (Rom. 5:12) and the federal head falls, entailing racial calamity and involving all his offspring beyond human reparation and restoration, the earth and creation send up a groan which continues to the present, for the groaning creation is destined to deliverance and to the display of God's purpose in the *coming days of the regeneration.*

When the fallen sons of Adam, by natural corruption and supernatural irruption, fill the earth with violence, God in mercy and justice sends deluge and destruction to preserve His purpose and His people in the earth (Gen. 6—8).

Upon the cleansed earth Noah and his sons go forth and at the conclusion of Genesis 10, which is the "Ethnological and Historical Record of the Nations" (Delitzsch), we read:

> These are the families of the sons of Noah, after their generations, in their nations; and by these were the nations divided in the *earth* after the flood (Gen. 10:32).

Then follows the scattering of the nations to their places on the habitable earth (Deut. 32:8), after which follows the

Call of Abraham

In the twelfth chapter of Genesis we see unfolded in detail the manner in which God called a solitary man out from the rest of the world "to become the head of an elect nation, destined throughout the long course of the world ages never again to mingle on equal terms with the rest of the world's stream." And this *choice in Abram* of *Israel* as the *One Nation* peculiar to His purpose was not a display of favoritism, of which there is none with God, but rather His choice in Israel was an object to a Divine end in view, for we read:

> Now the Lord had said unto Abram, Get thee out of thy country, and from thy kindred, and from thy father's house, unto a land that I will shew you; and I will make of thee a great nation, and I will bless thee and make thy name great, and thou shalt be a blessing; and I will bless them that bless thee, and curse him that curseth thee; and *in thee shall all families of the earth be blessed* (Gen. 12:1-3).

Thus our attention is still held to the *earth* and God's purpose in the earth.

After God's choice of the One Nation, Israel, we find choice after choice within this nation. "If Abram is called to give up his nationality, God will make of him a great nation; if his family, it is that all families may be blessed through him, and if he gives up his descent line and name, God will begin a new line in him and make his name great."

The *tribe* is chosen, the *family* within the tribe, the *house* and the *virgin* within the house; and when the Old Testament is brought to its close, the Law and the Prophets are awaiting fulfillment in the coming of Him who was the burden of their promise and prophecy.

Four hundred years of silence covering the period from Malachi to Matthew is broken by the advent of the promised Messiah to the House of David and the Nation of Israel. He was sent to bless Israel and through them the nations. His coming to them was God's plan for the world. Indeed, His coming to Israel was the Divine and destined way outlined in the program of prophecy by which the nations of the earth are blessed and the sovereignty of the earth passes into the hands of the Son of man.

The story of Messiah's reception by Israel is quickly told. "He came to *His own* (Israel), but His own *received Him not.*" He was delivered by them into the hands of Gentiles and without human cause He is put to death. It was the terrible death of the cross!

He arose from the dead and, in this resurrection from the dead, it is found He is not yet beyond Israel's call; and on the memorable day of Pentecost, Peter is selected and sent to call upon Israel to repent of this murder of Messiah. Peter assures them, in the great power of the Holy Ghost, that the "sure mercies of David" guarantees to them His return and their restoration and the restitution of all their national hopes (Acts 3:19, 21). Here, as often before, *they would not.*

Their ears are heavy, hearts dull, eyes blind, they will not convert and be healed.

Stephen's address in Acts 7 brings the national climax and crisis! They have not only slain the Messiah, but all that are "sent unto them." The blood of another son of Abraham is required of them! Unbelief has come to its full in this nation of the long-suffering God.

"As your fathers did, *so do ye,*" is the terrible indictment! It is all over! We have but to await till the record of the Acts comes to a conclusion to behold the nation judicially and temporarily set aside. God now turns attention to the Gentiles, and gives the official notice, as proclaimed in the book of Acts:

> Be it known therefore unto you, that the salvation of God is sent unto the Gentiles, and that they will hear it (Acts 28:28).

Until this time we have been tracing God's purpose for the *earth* through and in Israel.

We have not considered the *heavenlies;* indeed, since the mention of that sphere away back in Genesis, we have not thought of looking that way, so concerned have we been with

God's purpose for the earth.

To be sure, there has been an occasional glance directed towards the heavens, but as a place of contemplation and hope, and as a position to which our eyes are lifted, hearts centered and our destinies concerned—such has not been our consideration. We have now and then lifted our eyes to the aerial and stellar heavens, but *to heavenly places* far above all principality and power and might, and dominion, *where Christ is raised and seated,* this is a new sphere! It is all new and divergingly different!

Yet this is the place to which our attention is directed for the first time in the Scriptures and the direction comes to us from the Epistle to the Ephesians.

What does it all mean? Why are our thoughts thus taken from the earth and God's purpose therein and turned toward the *heavenlies?* Has God cast off His people whom He foreknew and abandoned His purpose on the earth? God forbid. There is a parenthesis in His purpose to be filled in, and this is the subject of the Ephesian Epistle.

Before we approach this "Alps of the New Testament" (A. T. Pierson) the writer greatly desires that each one of us would pray the prayer of the apostle Paul as recorded in Ephesians. Let us pray in humility:

That the God of our Lord Jesus Christ, the Father of Glory, may give unto you the Spirit of wisdom and revelation in the knowledge of Him: the eyes of your understanding being enlightened; that ye may know what is the hope of His calling, and what the riches of the glory of His inheritance in the saints. And what is the exceeding greatness of His power, to us-ward who believe, according to the working of His mighty power, which He wrought in Christ when He raised Him from the dead, and set Him at His own right hand in the heavenly places, far above all principality, and power, and might, and dominion, and every name that is named, not only in this world, but also in that which is to come. And hath put all things under His feet, and gave Him to be the Head over all things to the Church (Eph. 1:17-22).

2

THE CRISIS AND THE CHRIST

There might have been agitation, anxiety and terrible pertur-
bation of spirit when the claims of Christ were first presented and
brought into sharp conflict with previous convictions and
traditionary prepossessions, but the turmoil had subsided into
quiescent and immovable confidence in the Son of God.
—John Eadie, D.D., L.L.D., in *Ephesians.*

THE DAY OF Pentecost was fully come!

The Holy Spirit came from heaven!

The Gospels open with the advent of the Son of God from
heaven and the Book of Acts opens with the advent of the
Holy Spirit from heaven. The Holy Spirit of God had come
down to the earth because the Son of God had gone up to
heaven. The One came out because the Other had gone in.
Pentecost was what Dr. A. J. Gordon has beautifully and
significantly called "The birthday of the Holy Ghost."

As the Son of God had a day of coming into the world, so
also did the Spirit of God.

When the fullness of time was come *God sent His Son* (Gal.
4:4).

When the "day of Pentecost was fully come" *God sent His
Holy Spirit.* And certainly it is true that "as the presence of the
Son, exalting and revealing the Father, is the great fact of the
Gospels, so the presence of the Spirit, exalting and revealing
the Son, is the great fact of the Book of Acts." And the

method and ministry of the Son and the Spirit are likewise similar. As the *Son,* who came to reveal the Father, offered Himself first to Israel, so also the *Spirit,* who came to reveal the Son, offers Him first to Israel. This was the Divine order: "to the Jew first and also to the Greek."

In the Gospels, it is to the nation of *Israel first,* then the other nations (Matt. 10:6; 15:24).

In John's Gospel we behold the Son of God coming to His own people Israel, who reject Him (John 1:11, 12), and at the close of His ministry, He is sought by the Greeks (John 12:20).

In the Acts, as in the Gospels, the offer is to the Jew first, then to the Gentiles.

Peter's sermon at Pentecost follows this Divine order. Hear his first word:

> Ye men of *Judea* and all that dwell at *Jerusalem,* be this known unto *you* (Acts 2:14).

and again:

> Ye men of *Israel* hear these words (Acts 2:22).

Read again the record of Peter's second sermon and hear the conclusion. Addressing "ye men of Israel" (Acts 3:12), he says:

> Unto you first, God, having raised up His Son Jesus, sent Him to bless you, in turning away everyone of *you* from his iniquities (Acts 3:26).

Again a little later after the Gentiles had received and believed, we read:

> But when the Jews saw the multitudes, they were filled with envy, and spake against those things which were spoken by Paul, contradicting and blaspheming. Then Paul and Barnabas waxed bold, and said, it was necessary that the Word of God should first have been spoken to you: but seeing ye *put it from you,* and judge yourselves unworthy of everlasting life, lo we turn to the Gentiles. For so hath the Lord commanded us, saying, I have set thee to be

a light of the Gentiles, that thou shouldest be for salvation unto the ends of the earth (Acts 13:45-48).

But while the ministry of the Holy Spirit in the Book of Acts is to the Jew first, it is *also to the Greek,* and in chapter 10 we behold the kingdom of heaven opened unto the Gentiles. This is what C. I. Scofield calls "Peter's second use of the keys." (See *Scofield Reference Bible,* Acts 10.) This order in Acts is the Divine order. Blessing for the Gentiles succeeds the blessing of Israel. God has chosen Israel that in them He may bless the nations. Thus we see the ministry of the Book of Acts, which is divided unto Peter and Paul, is twofold, viz.:

1. To the Covenant People Israel,—the circumcision.

2. To the Strangers to the Covenants, the Gentiles,—the uncircumcision.

God had raised up an apostle whose office He magnified that they might minister to both the circumcision and the uncircumcision. This the early Church recognized.

When they saw that the gospel of the uncircumcision was committed unto me, as the gospel of the circumcision was unto Peter; (for he that wrought effectually in Peter to the apostleship of the circumcision, the same was mighty in me toward the Gentiles:) and when James, Cephas, and John, who seemed to be pillars, perceived the grace that was given unto me, they gave to me and Barnabas the right hands of fellowship; that we should go unto the heathen, and they unto the circumcision (Gal. 2:7-9).

This subject will be further considered in this our study of Ephesians under a division entitled, "The Liabilities of Israel" and "The Disabilities of the Gentiles."

But it must be remembered that the birthday of the Holy Spirit was also the *birthday* of the *Christian Church.* Here, again, the order was the Jew first and then the Gentile. The first members of the Church were Jews. The Gentiles were called afterward.

Throughout the Book of Acts we see a company of believing Jews and believing Gentiles, but nowhere in the

Book of Acts do we see national reception of Christ by any of the nations. Only *individuals* of the circumcision and individuals of the uncircumcision. In fact, only a remnant of either believed and received. This opportunity was afforded them both.

Dr. James H. Brookes had clear vision here, and in his invaluable work, *Israel and the Church,* he wrote:

> If Israel had repented and turned to God in obedience to the apostolic summons, their sins would have been blotted out, the millennial glory would have set in, the Lord Jesus would have returned from heaven, and restored the kingdom to Israel as the center of His earthly empire, and the channel of blessing to all other nations. This is what Peter taught, and what the Holy Spirit said through his mouth, as God lingered in tender mercy over Jerusalem, like the slowly departing glory in the days of Ezekiel. But Israel still rejected Him, and so heaven still received Him, and will continue to receive Him until the times of the restitution of all things.
>
> There is another passage, however, so perfectly clear in the light it throws upon the two already quoted, that it must remove every shadow of doubt concerning the future of Israel. For some time after the disclosure to which allusion has just been made, Peter was unable to look beyond the conversion of his own countrymen, in his zeal to hasten the crowning day of Christ, and it required a vision to convince him that his ascended Lord wished him to carry the Gospel to the Roman Centurion and to the Gentiles (Acts 10). Paul's commission, on the other hand, from the date of his remarkable conversion on the road to Damascus, embraced both divisions of the human race, for Jesus said of him to Ananias, "He is a chosen vessel unto Me, to bear My name before the Gentiles, the kings, and the children of Israel," the distinction between Jew and Gentile being still observed (Acts 9:15).

The Crisis and the Christ

It was at this point a seeming crisis was reached and a predicament presented. But God has never faced a crisis for He has always trusted in Christ! If we may say it reverently, God has never come to a panic for He has always worked to a purposed plan! No surprises have ever overtaken God in the administration of the ages that He should find it necessary to suddenly make contrivance to relieve Himself of sudden embarrassment. He is a sovereign God and in Him is all sufficiency!

From the time the Son took the first step in His humiliation and became the "first-born of all creation," He became the responsible trustee unto the Father, who placed the affairs of the ages in His hands!

The situation summarized is this: The Jew and the Gentile are *distinct*. This distinction is Divinely placed by God and what God has put asunder let no man join together. It is an offense not to distinguish between the *Jew, Gentile* and *Church of Christ* (1 Cor. 10:32).

It is equally an offense to each of them and the student should study to show himself "approved unto God, a workman that needeth not to be ashamed, rightly dividing the Word of Truth" (2 Tim. 2:15), so as to avoid giving offense to either or any of this triple division which God Himself has made.

The blessing of the Gentile nations depends upon Israel. Apart from Israel there is nothing for the nations. If Israel be set aside and a dispensation of judgment measured unto them, resulting in their removal from the land and the city, with David's throne in ruins, what can the believing Jew and the believing Gentile do? To whom shall they look? A remnant from the nation of Israel has believed and received Christ, but the nation is set aside for an age time judgment. A remnant from the Gentiles has believed and received but the nations must await Israel's recovery and blessing before they may have their portion, so dependent upon Israel.

What will be done? Oh the plenitude of God's purpose! *They are to be joined into one Body* in which they will neither be recognized as Jew nor Gentile, but *as one in Christ Jesus*. The middle wall of partition, which God Himself placed between them, is taken away. He abolished the enmity *to make in Himself one new man* and the foundation of this reconciliation of God into one Body, was the work of the cross (Eph. 2:14-16).

There Is No Crisis Where There Is Christ

The situation which seemed to be a crisis is not a crisis, lo, it is but a climax! A way was made for the dispensation now present without doing violence to former purpose or future performance!

It is not to be lightly considered that this bringing about this hitherto unheard-of union, between the Jew and the Gentile in the Church, was without the abrogation of God's former purpose in Israel and through them the blessing of the nations, according to the original promise to Abram, in the coming age!

His purpose in the future is unchanged, but here His program for the present is proclaimed. We are not a little grieved when now and then we hear persons who know nothing of the prophetic program, say: "God will have no special dealings with Israel in the future. He has included their national blessing in the Church as well as the rest of the nations."

The Church is not a movement for national blessing of either Jew or Gentile. It is an election from the nations. It does not include in its scope universal blessing, it is individual. Universal blessing for the earth is promised in Israel. The present dispensation is distinctive and any attempt to make it other, leads to a confusion and a tangle which can be cleared and corrected only by strict adherence to God's revealed purpose in this dispensation.

I tell you, the "but now in Christ Jesus" of Ephesians, does not set aside the "then shall the ransomed of the Lord return and come to Zion," of Isaiah!

Though the Ephesian Epistle leads us to the breadth and length and height and depth of God's purpose in the Church, we must turn aside to speak a word in behalf of Israel! The people of our prayers! While we contemplate our position in Christ we will not forget the people now in dispersion, whose scattering made possible our gathering!

God bless the nation which is now bearing Thy judgments while we are enjoying Thy grace, Amen!

We shall trace the triumph of God in the dispensation now present and shall behold the priority of God's purpose in the Church. Ephesians is the Book of the grace of God, and we will discover that the merits of the Jew and the demerits of the Gentile do not interfere with God's display of grace, for grace is apart from either!

3

THE STRUCTURE OF THE EPISTLE

> One of the mountain peaks of Revelation, disclosing the
> ultimate and crowning purposes of God in Christ and in the
> Church. As usual with Saint Paul, the great division is Doctrinal
> (1—3), and Practical (4—6), the latter following as the necessary
> and inevitable consequence of the former.
> —Dr. W. H. Griffith Thomas in *Methods of Bible Study.*

IN THE PRECEDING chapter we considered "The Crisis and
Christ," and came to the assurance that there is no crisis where
there is Christ! Though Israel was at a national crisis, and
because of their default, the Gentile nations were with them,
placed on the waiting list for final and full blessing. Notwith-
standing, this very crisis gave opportunity for the publication
of a number on the program of God, hitherto unpublished, viz.,
The union of Jew and Gentile in one body—"builded together
for an habitation through the Spirit."

"Known unto God are all His works *from* the beginning of
the world," but this purpose had its origin "in Him" *before* the
foundation of the world. Praise be to the Lord! This is too high
for our vision and too deep for our comprehension, but these
are the certain facts of revelation.

Before beginning the exposition of the Epistle to the
Ephesians, we shall study its structure, that we may better
understand its subject and scope. The following outline is a
suggestive summary of the Epistle:

PART 1
INTRODUCTION
1:1, 2

PART 2
THE CALLING OF THE CHURCH
1:3—3:21

PART 3
THE CONDUCT OF THE CHURCH
4:1—6:9

PART 4
THE CONFLICT OF THE CHURCH
6:10-20

CONCLUSION
6:21-24

The three main divisions of the epistle may be seen at a glance, and each of the three divisions are to be interpreted in the light of the sphere revealed in 1:3, viz.: "the heavenlies." A heavenly *Calling* demands heavenly *Conduct* and assures heavenly *Conflict*.

For those who study Bible Books by chapters we furnish the following *Key Words:*

Chapter 1	Key word:	Redemption (vv. 1-7)
Chapter 2	Key word:	Reconciliation (v. 16)
Chapter 3	Key word:	Revelation (v. 3)
Chapter 4	Key word:	Walk (v. 1)
Chapter 5	Key word:	Worship (vv. 19, 20)
Chapter 6	Key word:	Warfare (vv. 11, 12)

In Chapter 1 of Ephesians, under the subject of *Redemption,* the Bible student may wish to make notes in the margin of the Bible as follows:

Persons ...... "us" .... (v. 3)
Position ...... "in Christ" .... (v. 3)
Place .... "the Heavenlies" .... (v. 3)
Purpose ...... "Eternal" .... (v. 4)
Pleasure ...... "His will" .... (v. 5)
Praise .... "Glory of His grace" .... (v. 6)
Power .... "Mighty power" .... (v. 19)
Point .... "far above all" .... (v. 21)

In Chapter 2 concerning *Reconciliation,* there are certain interesting notations also, namely:

Dead in sins .... (v. 1)
Disobedience to God .... (v. 2)
Deliverance by grace .... (vv. 4, 5)
Display in ages to come .... (vv. 9, 10)

We behold here (1) The Old Condition (vv. 1-3), (2) The New Position (vv. 5, 6), (3) The Future Exhibition (v. 7), (4) The Present Admonition (vv. 8-10).

Notice, "in times past Gentiles in the flesh" (2:12), in contrast with "but now in Christ Jesus" (2:13).

The second chapter of Ephesians may be divided after this manner:

The Condition of the Jew and Gentile (vv. 1-10).
The Position of the Jew and Gentile (vv. 11-22).

These notations and alliterations are given for meditation, but they will be found true to interpretation.

In Chapter 3, the key word of which is *Revelation,* we notice first:

Paul the
Prisoner and the   }   (3:1-3)
Purpose

We are introduced to the Messenger and inducted into the Mystery; and in the following manner, this may be impressed on, and retained by, the memory:

```
Messenger  ...............  (3:1, 7)
Message    ...............  (3:6)
Mystery    ...............  (3:8, 9)
Measurements  ...........  (3:18)
```

Note Chapter 4. Phibbs and Trench give to chapters 4, 5 and 6 the following titles: 4. Endowment, 5. Enduement, 6. Equipment. The student will do well to note these excellent words summarizing successfully the contents of this division of Ephesians.

For your Christian life we suggest the student notice the occurrence of the word *not.*

Walk not	(v. 17)	Conduct
Talk not	(v. 22)	Conversation
Sin not	(v. 26)	Circumspection
Grieve not	(v. 30)	Provocation

Notice the word *let:*

Let him that stole steal no more, but rather

Let him labor (v. 28).

Let no corrupt communication proceed from your mouth (v. 29).

Let bitterness and wrath be put away (v. 31).

The contents of chapter 4 may well be summed up as follows:

The Worthy Walk } of the { Heavenly Hope

In Chapter 5, the key word is *worship.* This chapter has for its general subject, *Christ and the Church.* There are nine things He has done and does for His Church:

```
                    loved
                    gave Himself for
                    sanctifies
    CHRIST          cleanses              CHURCH
                    washes
                    presents
                    preserves
                    nourishes
                    cherishes
```

Ephesians, chapter 5, verses 25 to 27.

In Chapter 6, the key word is *warfare.* We are still with the *family* in verses 1 to 5, and are receiving instruction for children, for fathers, reaching in the household to the inclusion of servants. At verse 10, we reach the Apostle's "finally" and at verse 11, we enter the "fight." It is in this chapter we learn that we are equipped with "armament" and we're advised of our "adversary." The *place of the Conflict is in the heavenlies* and the people of the conflict; "we" and "principalities and powers" (v. 12).

We behold the Divine panoply for protection. We are prepared for the contest and assured of the conquest.

A splendid summary of this chapter may be thus displayed:

The   Sphere of the } and the { Weapons of the
      Struggle   Warfare

Thus we have supplied the student with *key words* and *contents phrases* which we believe will prove very suggestive. We do not urge chapter study of any book of the Bible, for we well know that the chapter divisions are not inspired of God and are only an arrangement for convenience. Many are unhappy with the chapter divisions, and they who are determined to study the Bible by chapters will oftentimes lose sight of the Spirit's design and division of the book. There is spiritual symmetry in the scope of each book of the Bible, as there is in the sum total of all the books into one Book, the Bible!

PART 2
The Calling of the Church
Ephesians 1:3—3:21

4

THE CALLING OF THE CHURCH
Ephesians 1:1-3

The Epistle overflows with lofty thoughts and doctrines. He writes it from prison at Rome. Things which he scarcely anywhere else utters, he here expounds.
—St. Chrysostom, Preamble to his *Homilies on Epistle to the Ephesians.*

Paul, an apostle of Jesus Christ by the will of God, to the saints which are at Ephesus, and to the faithful in Christ Jesus: Grace be to you, and peace, from God our Father, and from the Lord Jesus Christ (Ephesians 1:1, 2).

Introduction

THESE SALUTATORY sentences are indeed full and fertile! We behold at first the human author and at once the persons addressed but back and beyond all, the power and the person,—"the will of God." The *origin* is the Divine will of God, the *organ* is the apostle Paul, and the *object,* "Saints and faithful in Christ Jesus."

The message of Ephesians is *initially* in the will of God, *inclusively* to those in the Son of God, *instrumentally* by Paul the servant of God and *ultimately* to all the "saints of God."

Behold the threefold fact of revelation, viz.: Predestination, Designation and Destination, (Detailed in Chapter 7).

There is here no circuitous excursion in search of a starting point, for instantly we are directed to the primary cause— "The will of God!" "The will of God" is the source and spring of all! The Book of Genesis opens with the words, "In the beginning God created," etc., and we are introduced to the Person and the Power of God in *His work,* but, in Ephesians, it is the Person and Purpose of God in *His will.* The will of God is the ground and background of all revelation and manifestation. The Sovereign will of a Sovereign God antedating all time and originating all things! The Gospel leaves no place for human willing and human working, because human will and human work had no part in its purpose or plan. Its origination, manifestation and consummation is with God. We desire to lay deep and well our foundations now; for later in our study of this Epistle, we desire to shout and cry aloud without intimidation, "by grace are ye saved, through faith and that not of yourselves, it is the *gift of God.*" Ephesians fixes the point where all human boasting is excluded—it is—"the will of God."

The salvation we preach begins in God, is continued by God, and comes to its consummation in God.

If hereinafter we are to behold the *work of Christ,* it is by *the will of God.*

If it be the *walk of the saints,* it is by *the will of God.* Outside the will of God there is no one or no thing—such is the message of Ephesians.

The "will of God" will occur again and again in Ephesians. ("His will" 1:5, 9, 11, etc.) While in verse 1 the Apostle's call is by the will of God, it is but the introduction of "His will" which will be ever confronting and comforting us. In fact when we read Ephesians, we think often of Paul's words to the Corinthians—"And all things are of God" (2 Cor. 5:18). Surely in Ephesians, "all things are of God." Notice "His will" (1:3), "His grace," (v. 6), "His good pleasure" (v. 9), "His glory" (v. 14), "His calling" (v. 18), "His inheritance" (v. 18), "His power" (v. 19), "His mighty power" (v. 19), "His own right hand" (v. 20), "His feet" (v. 22), "His Body" (v. 23).

How many things are "His" and all of these things are because of "His will."

The above are the things which are "His" in chapter 1. The student may follow further at leisure.

At verse 2 we face a word to be fully and freely considered in the body of the Epistle, viz.: "grace." Stier remarks that in the two expressions in verse 2, "grace" and "peace," we have trace of the two divisions of the Epistle—"God's grace towards us and our faith towards Him."—Henry Alford.

The initiative and the issue are both here—"grace" from God—"peace" for us. Study here something of the Divine distance bridged by God. "Grace" and "peace" from God and the Father and the Lord Jesus Christ to *you*. Can anything but God's grace reach such an infinite distance and bring "peace" to such as "you"? Who is sufficient and who is required to span such a gulf to bring such a peace? "The Lord Jesus Christ."

Where is the measuring line to mark off the distance between the *Father* and the *Son* and the *sinner?* Between God and the sinner is the Cross! Tell the distance if you can. By the expiation of the Cross is the impartation of peace.

Surely G. Campbell Morgan has well said:

> Grace is the river flowing from the heart of God. Peace is the resulting consciousness of the filling of the heart of the trusting soul. The river and the peace alike come from the Lord Jesus Christ.

We are now ready for the *parsing* of the most wonderful sentence in the world of words and speech. Beginning at verse 3 and continuing to the close of verse 14 is *one sentence*.

> Blessed be the God and Father of our Lord Jesus Christ, who hath blessed us with all spiritual blessings in heavenly places in Christ: According as He hath chosen us in Him before the foundation of the world, that we should be holy and without blame before Him in love: Having predestinated us unto the adoption of children by Jesus Christ to Himself, according to the good pleasure of His will. To the praise of the glory of His grace, wherein He hath made us accepted in the Beloved: In whom we have redemption through His Blood, the forgiveness of sins, according to the riches of His grace; Wherein He hath abounded toward us in all wisdom and prudence; Having made known unto

us the mystery of His will, according to His good pleasure which He hath purposed in Himself: That in the dispensation of the fulness of times He might gather together in one all things in Christ, both which are in heaven, and which are on earth; even in Him: In whom also we have obtained an inheritance, being predestinated according to the purpose of Him who worketh all things after the counsel of His own will: That we should be to the praise of His glory, who first trusted in Christ. In whom ye also trusted, after that ye heard the Word of Truth, the Gospel of your salvation: in whom also, after that ye believed, ye were sealed with that Holy Spirit of promise, Which is the earnest of our inheritance until the redemption of the purchased possession, unto the praise of His glory (Eph. 1:3-14).

We recently picked up a school-girl's notebook marked "Language," and read this statement: "Never use over thirty words in one sentence." Thirty words seem to be about as many as man can correlate into one sentence and display any sense. Beyond thirty words, according to the theory of the educators, man is not intelligible. In an attempt to string more than thirty words together it has been proven that man fails to clearly express himself, or impress others. If use is made of more than thirty words, punctuation is called into service, and punctuation often introduces complication. When man's tongue continues to carry conversation beyond his brain's conception he becomes a glibbering fool! This may be true of human writings, but not of the Divine oracles. Man reasons but God reveals and indeed vast is the difference between human reason and Divine revelation.

Thirty words, the scope of a human sentence, but in this sentence of Divine utterance, there are two hundred and sixty-four words! The greatest single sentence known in all the literature of the world! The *Logos* of God! The ultimate and the utmost in scope and scale! A sentence which rises from argument to doxology and in which logic swells into lyrics!

A sentence which originates in the Blessed God (v. 3) and terminates in, to the "praise of His glory" (v. 14).

Wonderful sentence of Ephesians! And much like the Book

itself, scaling heights and spanning breadths unknown! John Eadie calls this sentence a "Magnificent Anthem."

The study of it will reveal great grammatical construction. One truth will, in this sentence, give birth to another, all bound together in "philosophical precision" and by the laws of powerful association.

This sentence is as "a wheel within a wheel," complete yet always coming to completion. The sentence is built upon a series of participles, each participle adding another link to the chain, until, as it were, all is forged.

The scope of the sentence is from one eternity to another! It reaches from before the foundation of the world to the consummation of the ages. There is the elaboration of every great truth of revelation in this one sentence.

What depth of revelation awaits our meditation!

> Following closely upon the introductory benediction, and connected with it, the subject of the Church's heavenly calling is entered upon. The first three chapters of this Epistle may thus be named: (1) Predestination, or the Church's Origin, (2) Edification, or the Church's Construction, (3) Vocation, or the Church's Function.
>
> —G. Campbell Morgan, at Mundsley, 1909.

Parsing the Sentence

At the opening of the first main division of the Book of Ephesians, "The Calling of the Church" (1:3—3:21), is the beginning of the most wonderful of all sentences and to which we referred previously. This sentence in the Greek Testament, extends from verse 3 to and including verse 14 of the first chapter, and it contains *Two Hundred and Sixty-four Words!*

A sentence which we declare to be a summary of every great truth of revelation. (We do not say prophecy, but revelation, for there are subjects in the New Testament of which Old Testament prophets knew nothing.)

We are now ready for the parsing of this wonderful sentence in which we are to behold the "Calling of the Church" and the purpose, power and perfection of God in the same. This subject is too great for us. Unto God we look. This is His Book!

Verses 3 and 4

What Divine difference and distinction there is between the calling of Israel and the calling of the Church. Nowhere is it seen in such sharp contrast as in these two verses. The character of the calling of the Church is such as to require a careful consideration on the part of the student; indeed, it is necessary to the understanding of this Epistle which is the "Alps of the New Testament," and in which, as Chrysostom says, "Things which the Apostle scarcely anywhere else utters, he here expounds." Perhaps these striking facts may be emphasized in the following manner:

1. The Source of the Calling .. "God" .... (v. 3)
2. The Subject of the Calling .. "Us' .... (v. 3)
3. The Scope of the Calling ... "Spiritual blessings" .. (v. 3)
4. The Sum of the Calling .... "All" .... (v. 3)
5. The Sphere of the Calling .. "Heavenly places" ... (v. 3)
6. The Standing of the Called . "In Christ" .... (v. 3)

We shall follow, in order, each of the above.

1. The Source of the Calling: "God"

"Blessed be the God and Father of our Lord Jesus Christ." God is here called "blessed." The adjective in the doxology is placed before the substantive because it is used as a predicate and this formula occurs at least thirty times in the Old Testament. The word "blessed" occurs eight times in the New Testament (Mark 14:61; Luke 1:68; Rom. 1:25; 9:5; 2 Cor. 1:3; 11:31; Eph. 1:3; 1 Pet. 1:3). It is said that an examination of these passages will reveal that the word "blessed" is always used of God and never of man (Morgan). It is the "God and Father of our Lord Jesus Christ," while in the Old Testament, the Synoptic Gospels and the Acts, (first half particularly) it is the "God of Abraham, Isaac and Jacob" or "the God of our fathers."

A reference to the concordance will reveal the oft occurrence of these titles in both Testaments. They are titles used to signify the Covenant relationship of God to Israel. The absence of these titles in the later Epistles of Paul is not without signification.

Peter in his first Post-Pentecostal address uses the double title and says, "The God of Abraham and of Isaac and of Jacob, the God of our fathers" (Acts 3:13). In a Book where there is not a superfluous word, and in a Book which is not a book of synonyms, there is *a difference* between the "God of our fathers" and the "God and Father of our Lord Jesus Christ."

We must remember that the names and *titles* of God the Father and the Son, are personal, official and dispensational. They who overlook these titles will never know much truth. If the reference is to the Scriptures, then the question, "What's in a name?" means much. "The God and Father of our Lord Jesus Christ." What a revelation in this relation. This is the highest of titles—the God and Father of our Lord Jesus Christ! Notice the threefold fullness, Lord—Jesus—Christ. To be the God and Father of our Lord Jesus Christ is God's highest honor and full revelation of Himself. It is not here the Covenant relation He bears to Abraham, Isaac and Jacob, but that *filial* relation as the God and Father of the Lord Jesus Christ. It is the God and Father of our Lord Jesus Christ who hath blessed "us." As the God of Abraham, Isaac and Jacob He enters into covenant with Israel for their national perpetuity and blessing and through them, blessing for the Gentile nations of the earth; but He is the God and Father of "our" Lord Jesus Christ, and this establishes our calling and blessing at its source!

An old Scotch saint, when asked if she did not presume upon God when she insisted on the assurance of her salvation, said: "My salvation was an eternal arrangement between God the Father and His Son and they who *counselled* it and *commenced* it will *continue* and *conclude* it." Christ was the oracle of God before there was order or oath. He who afterward swore in an oath unto Abraham, is He who said, "before Abraham was *I am*."

2. The Subject of the Calling: "Us"

"He hath blessed 'us'." It is not always easy to distinguish in Ephesians between the "we," the "ye," the "us" and the "ours." We believe these little words mean much to the interpretation of the Epistle.

The "us," we are confident, is used by the Spirit of God in reference to the Jew and Gentile as united in one Body in Christ, and this is the subject of the Ephesian letter. By the "us," the "we," and the "ye" the Jew, the Gentile and the Church of God are distinguished and this distinction is of primary importance to the study of Ephesians or any other portion of Scripture. What God has separated let no man join together. Surely our beloved Dr. C. I. Scofield has faithfully shown in his little book, *Rightly Dividing the Word of Truth,* the confusion introduced when this threefold division of the Scriptures is not observed.

The "us" is a reference to both Jew and Gentile who, in Christ Jesus, are not now reckoned as either, for in the Church there is neither Jew nor Gentile, male nor female, bond nor free. They are now both brought together in a place, where "neither circumcision availeth anything or uncircumcision, but a *new creation.*" Many to whom we now write are included in this "us," if so be they are in Christ.

We desire to include here a valuable note from the pen of Dr. W. H. Griffith Thomas in his remarkable book, *The Holy Spirit of God.* Dr. Thomas wrote:

> It should not be forgotten that Ephesians is the next place in the New Testament, after Matthew, where the Church universal, as distinct from the Church local, is treated (Page 271).
>
> The idea of all believers being one in Christ is evident from the first, but it is only in the Epistle to the Ephesians that we find it receiving full expression and adequate treatment (Page 172).
>
> The Epistle to the Romans deals mainly and primarily with the relation of the individual to God in Christ. The Epistle to the Ephesians, on the other hand, starts from the corporate side of

Christianity, and views the individual as one of the Body (Pages 172-3).

Dr. Griffith Thomas sees where many stumble, and as the above statements receive further treatment by him, we will quote yet more in future studies.

3. The Scope of the Calling: "Spiritual Blessings"

"Who hath blessed us with all spiritual blessings." And here again the distinction between the Calling of the Church is in conclusive contrast with the Calling of Israel and the Gentiles. The scope of the Church's blessing is "spiritual," while that of Israel was temporal and material. Such blessings as the temporal and material were of "frequent promise in Mosaic and Messianic Scriptures—the dew of heaven, the fatness of the earth, abundance of corn, wine and oil, peace, longevity and a flourishing household."—John Eadie.

Perhaps in no other place is the character of Israel's blessings so succinctly summarized as in Deuteronomy 32:13, 14:

> He made him ride on the high places of the earth, that he might eat the increase of the fields; and he made him to suck honey out of the rock, and oil out of the flinty rock; butter of kine, and milk of sheep, with fat of lambs, and rams of the bread of Bashan, and goats, with the fat of kidneys of wheat; and thou didst drink the pure blood of the grape.

But in Ephesians, temporal blessings have taken the subordinate place. In Ephesians, we look not at things which are seen, they are temporal and tangible, but at the eternal things which are held up and out for the discernment of the eye of faith.

When the sun rises, the stars that sparkled during the night are eclipsed by the flood of superior brilliance, and disappear, but still keep their places; so here in Ephesians, the earthly blessings of Israel are dimmed and discounted by those of a dispensation now present with its new purpose for a new people, a new place, in a new position!

Eadie and Moule both agree that the New Testament warrants us in saying that these blessings are termed "spiritual" from their connection with the Holy Spirit. The study of the Holy Spirit in Ephesians, will add luster to this statement.

4. The Sum of the Calling: "All ... Blessings"

Here blessing in freeness comes to fullness and finality. It is the all-including comprehensive word "all" which is used often by Paul in his prison letters and especially in Colossians.

"All!" The circle is complete and nothing is wanted! No conditioned blessings but all conferred blessings. Not, as Israel's restricted and bounded blessings depending upon their faithfulness, but all the blessings promised are secured by the faithfulness of One, in whom we have all things and of whom are all things.

5. The Sphere of the Calling: "Heavenly Places"

Blessed with all spiritual blessings in "heavenly places." Having seen the *totality* of blessings we now come to the *locality* of the blessing. "Heavenly places" in contrast with earthly places. God's purpose for the earth is in Israel, but His purpose for the "heavenlies" is to be realized in and through the Church.

"In heavenly places" is literally, "in the heavenlies," an adjective without a noun. The name is rightly supplied in the A. V. Says Moule, "The form of the adjective suggests not only a heavenly origin, but a heavenly locality."* With this, virtually, the best scholars of all ages agree. This is as much a locality as God gave Israel, except that it is as boundless as theirs was bounded. "Heavenlies" is not a figure of speech, but a place in space; not an adaptation of a spiritual principle, but a habitation for a spiritual people. The phrase occurs four other times in this Epistle (1:20; 2:6; 3:10; 6:13), and the

---

*H. C. G. Moule, *Studies in Ephesians* (Grand Rapids: Kregel Publications, 1977), p. 45.

reference is in each instance to a *locality.* We not only have our *wealth* in the heavenlies but subsequent study will reveal that our *witness* and *warfare* is confined to the same sphere.

The sphere of our calling is in the heavenlies. The possession God gave Israel was marked out and measured off. Said God to Abraham, "Unto thy seed have I given this land, from the river of Egypt unto the great river, the river Euphrates" (Gen. 15:18).

The calling of Israel was related to a land the Lord gave to them. The very locality itself was chosen for the ministry God had laid upon Israel. "When the Most High divided to the nations their inheritance, when He separated the sons of Adam, He set the bounds of the people according to the number of the children of Israel." Behold the Divine logic of the locality.

When Israel remained faithful and in the land, they exercised their Divinely given vocation. God's choice and calling of the Church to the heavenlies is to exercise a ministry in that locality, and the Church is of little or no use in any other place. This will come under our consideration at other times.

6. The Standing of the Called: "In Christ"

What position is this? A standing in the land? No. A standing before the nations? No. A standing in the righteousness of the law? No. A standing in the "Fathers" after the flesh? No. A standing in circumcision, covenants or carnal commandments? No—but *a standing in Christ!* The calling is to the heavenlies and the standing is in Him who is now rejected from the earth and retained in the heavens. The Church is as much rejected and separated from the earth as is Christ the Head. The Church as "in Christ" is likewise "with Christ." It is a very foolish thing for the Church to attempt to establish herself on the earth when she is *called with Christ in the heavenlies.* This position presupposes the work of the cross when we died with Christ; the power of the resurrection when we were raised with Christ: and these are the subject of

Romans, but Ephesians continues the Gospel and adds: "He hath raised us up together and made us sit together with Christ in heavenly places." This is our position who were once Jews and Gentiles but are *now one* in Christ Jesus.

We have thus briefly outlined the Divine difference and distinction in the calling of the Church and the calling of Israel. These are but suggestions which will be carried to a further and fuller consideration in succeeding studies. We have sought to discover the Purpose of Our Calling, now we shall next consider the Priority of Our Calling (v. 4).

O God, Thy Divine blessings and benefactions are beyond and above our understanding! We are dependent upon Thy revelation for all information. Thy ways are past our finding out, but not past Thy revealing! Amen.

5

THE PRIORITY OF THE CALLING

Ephesians 1:4-14

Before the foundation of the world. That expression shows we
have nothing to do with this world—we only pass through it. The
earthly people are chosen from the foundation of the world (Rev.
13:8; Matt. 25:34) the heavenly people before the world began.
God thought of us before He thought of Israel, and yet we hear of
Israel first.

—William Lincoln in *Ephesians*.

IN THE PARSING of this wonderful sentence (1:3-14) we have
discovered something of the "Purpose of God's Calling of the
Church." We now seek to better understand the "Priority of
the Calling." In verse 4 (chap. 1) we read:

According as He hath chosen us in Him before the foundation
of the world, that we should be holy and without blame before
Him in love (Eph. 1:4).

The word "according" which occurs here is used frequently
throughout the Epistle. Sixteen times the Greek word is used
with but slight variation in one instance and that in the word
as used here. The word "according" occurs five times in this
wonderful sentence, viz.: 1:4, 5, 7, 9, 11. In this instance the
word is the adverb *kathos* and defines the connection of this
verse with the preceding.

The word "according" as used in this Epistle indicates
comparison and consequence. It is a resultant word. An

established cause results in consequence. As used in Ephesians and especially in this sentence it is pivotal and connecting. The word as used in this sentence is the *very key to its contents,* for the word "according" *explains* what has gone before and *expands* that which comes after. What is enfolded is by this word unfolded, and what is determined is by this word developed. It is a word used in the process of the evolution of revelation!

The word as used in this sentence (1:3-14) is its very key, for it explains that which immediately precedes it, and expands the same in what immediately follows. It is the key to the construction of the sentence and the key to its instruction. This sentence unfolds its meaning and moves to its climax at the close of verse 14, all by the means of this word "according."

Each use of the word "according" demands another, until all is accomplished and all things have reached their goal—"the praise of His Glory" (v. 14).

Not without great significance are the words of Eadie in referring to this sentence:

> Each suggesting the other by a law of powerful association ... one truth instinctively gives birth to the other.

For example, in verse 3 we are introduced to the sphere to which the Church is called, namely, "heavenly places" or a supermundane sphere. Now the *place* of the calling demands the *priority* of the calling. If the place to which the Church is called is supermundane, is it not to be expected that the time of the calling was premundane or "before the foundation of the world"? The "according" here reveals the cause and consequence in perfect concord. It shows the harmony of the purpose, the place, and the position.

The calling of Israel was for an earthly ministry and Israel was chosen *"from* the foundation of the world" (Matt. 25:34), but the calling of the Church is unto the "heavenlies" and for a ministry in that sphere, therefore choice is made, *"before* the foundation of the world."

The words "from" and "before" differ vastly in meaning. If this distinction were unnoticed in common communication and conversation, to what extent would confusion prevail? Will less confusion be introduced in the Scriptures if these words are not thus distinguished? Certainly a thing done "*before* the foundation of the world" is not identical with a thing done "*from* the foundation of the world."

The Church was chosen in Him before the foundation of the world and this premundane calling presupposes a supermundane ministry. In Matthew's Gospel we learn of wisdom kept secret "*from*" the foundation of the world (Matt. 13:25), but here is purpose and predestination prior to that. "Before the foundation of the world" occurs three times in the New Testament; besides its use in this verse (4), it occurs in John 17:24 and First Peter 1:20. Three things are declared to have obtained before the foundation of the world:

1. The Love of the Father for the Son (John 17:24)

2. The Choice of the Church in Him (Eph. 1:4)

3. The Foreordination of Redemption by the Blood of the Lamb (1 Pet. 1:19, 20)

These three things lie back beyond all historical manifestation and are the subject of *subsequent revelation*.

O, beloved believer in Christ, whether Jew or Gentile after the flesh now one in Christ Jesus, could there be a subject so transcendingly great and gracious, surprising and startling as that we were chosen in Christ before the "foundation of the world" and simultaneously with the display of the filial love of the Father for the Son and the foundation of Redemption in the foreordination of the Sacrifice?

Jesus looked unto the Father and said, "Father, Thou lovest Me before the foundation of the world." So may we who are "in Christ" look unto the God and Father of our Lord Jesus Christ and say, "Father, Thou lovest us, and made choice of us, before the foundation of the world." Redemption was accomplished in God's sight, "before the foundation of the world" and we were chosen contemporaneously with the foreordination of the Sacrifice! "Such thoughts are too wonderful for me!" You say, something to think about? Yea, rather something to cause thanks and trust, wonder and worship!

This phrase itself declares that this election and selection is no act of time, for time dates from the creation, though some would have us believe the word "foundation" means *irruption*. This, however, has not been successfully established or substantiated.

"*From* the foundation of the world," says Moule, "means apparently since the beginning of *human* time."* But with the word "before," as here, the context always suggests the highest reference; "before any created being began."

The generic idea is therefore what Olshausen calls "Zeit-losigkeit," timelessness, implying, of course, absolute eternity.

Believers need not be in ignorance as to their relationship to this present world, for certainly a people chosen before the foundation of the world and to a future ministry in the "heavenlies" (Eph. 3:10), in which place they are now positionally viewed in Christ, are not, in the harmony and nature of things, to expect a portion, position and place in this world. There is a suggestive simplicity in the words of William Lincoln: "This world is something like a hotel, where people put up for a little time. We are going home."

As the *time* of Israel's calling secures unto them the place of their calling—the earth; so the *timelessness* of the calling of the Church marks out the earthlessness of its ministry and the sphere of its ministration. While the things here suggested are crowding upon us for consideration, we must withhold until chapter 3 and verse 10 is reached.

Man is never found in a fossil state or among prehistoric remains. We are well aware that Divine revelation has

---

*H. C. G. Moule, *Studies in Ephesians* (Grand Rapids: Kregel Publications, 1977), p. 46.

anticipated and antedated human science. Science is what thinks; Revelation is what *God knows*. Science is the result of *man's knowledge;* while Revelation is the publishing of *God's foreknowledge.* Science is discovery and recovery on the part of man, but Revelation begins at the source and foretells the succession of things. Genesis 1:1 is the *original creation* and Genesis 1:3 is the *beginning of recreation.* Between these there is a dateless parenthesis.

Whatever of fossil remains may be discovered or uncovered, regardless of the evidence of antiquity the same may bear, they cannot antedate and out-date the provision made in the Holy Scriptures. There is no such thing in the material universe as a pre-historic specimen. This term is but an accommodation for man's limitation.

There is in existence some evidence of vegetable and animal life which existed prior to the cosmic order of the world that "now is," and antedating the occupation of this earth by Adam's race, which was but a few thousand years ago, but of pre-historic times the Bible does not admit. There is nothing to antedate the "beginning," when God created the heavens and the earth (Gen. 1:1).

Geology cannot get back of Genesis, and certainly astronomy is not dependent on Adam or his race. Events preceding the world that now is, and the advent of Adam and his race, are not omitted from history, for the Divine historian has in Genesis 1:1 and 2 given record of the same. While the record is brief, it is complete. In subsequent Scriptures it is developed somewhat, but these things do not constitute the subject matter of the Bible, which is mainly concerned with the unfolding of Salvation's purpose and plan with man. Again we say, there is no history of which the Bible does not take cognizance.

Now and then a scare headline in a daily paper announces the discovery of a "pre-historic man." Let there be no cause for alarm, for man is never found in a fossil state. Man is historic, not pre-historic. The creation of man is contemporaneous with the recreation and reordering of the original creation which had undergone a "cataclysmic change as the result of Divine judgment." The record of this reordering and recreation begins with verse 3 of Genesis 1.

Dr. C. I. Scofield, in the *Scofield Reference Bible,* has simplified the matter after this manner:

The Original Creation (Genesis 1:1)

In the beginning God created the heaven and the earth.

The Earth Made Waste and Empty by Judgment (Genesis 1:2, Jeremiah 4:23-26)

And the earth was without form, and void; and darkness was upon the face of the deep. And the Spirit of God moved upon the face of the waters (Gen. 1:2).

I beheld the earth, and, lo, it was without form, and void; and the heavens, and they had no light. I beheld the mountains, and, lo, they trembled, and all the hills moved lightly. I beheld, and lo, there was no man, and all the birds of the heavens were fled. I beheld, and, lo, the fruitful place was a wilderness, and all the cities thereof were broken down at the presence of the Lord, and by his fierce anger (Jer. 4:23-26).

The New Beginning—the First Day; Light Diffused (Genesis 1:3-5)

And God said, Let there be light: and there was light ... And God called the light Day, and the darkness He called Night. And the evening and the morning were the first day.

But Ephesians reveals a Pre-historic *Person*, a Pre-historic *Purpose* with a Pre-historic *Plan* involving a Pre-historic *Choice.*

We were "chosen in Him before the foundation of the world." Revealed history began with the "foundation of the world" (Gen. 1:1). We were chosen in Him prior to this time. Spiritually speaking, we, members of the Body of Christ, are pre-historic specimens of His grace and goodness, purpose and plan. The priority of our choice and calling leaves no cohering point for human calculation and is beyond explanation other than this, that it is "according to the good pleasure of His will."

What Thou hast done and why, we know not now, O God, but we shall know hereafter. *We dare not, and do not ask why or wherefore? We only ask that the eyes of our understanding may be opened, that we may understand the "hope of His calling." Amen.*

6

THE PREDESTINED PURPOSE
OF THE CALLING

Ephesians 1:4-6

Beware of the miserable hendiadys, "His glorious grace," by which all the richness and depth of meaning are lost. The end, God's end, in our predestination to adoption is that the glory— glorious nature, brightness and majesty, and kindliness and beauty,—of His grace might be an object of men and angels' praise; both as it is in Him, infinite and ineffable and infinite,— and exemplified in *us,* its objects.

—Henry Alford.

HAVING CONSIDERED the "Priority of the Calling," we must now proceed to the consideration of "The Predestined Purpose of the Calling."

According as He hath chosen us in Him before the foundation of the world, that we *should be holy and without blame* before Him in love: having predestinated us unto the adoption of children by Jesus Christ to Himself, *according to the good pleasure of His will,* to the praise of the *glory of His grace* (Eph. 1:4-6).

The predestined purpose of the calling may be readily seen by the emphasized portions of the above verses. Let us now notice three things:

1. "That we should be holy and without blame before Him in love"
2. "According to the good pleasure of His will"
3. "To the praise of the glory of His grace"

With spiritual illumination and joyful anticipation let us consider these things.

1. "That we should be holy and without blame before Him in love" (v. 4)

The result of this calling of the believer is that "we should be holy and without blame before Him in love." That we should be *holy?* What manner of language is this,—we holy? We, who were born in sin and conceived in iniquity, holy? Yes, it is as actual as it is astonishing. Sometimes when good news overtakes and overwhelms us we say, "Well, I can hardly believe my own ears." But here we are not asked to believe any of our senses, but to believe God's Word! "That we should be holy and without blame before Him in love," is what it says.

There are two things here mentioned, viz.: (1) our state and (2) our standing. In state we are "holy," our standing is "before Him." But think, we who were once hopeless are now "holy." "Holy and without blame." With slight variation the two adjectives express the same idea. The first concerns *principle* and the second *practice*. A holy nature leads to a stainless life. It is the uniform teaching of the Apostle that holiness is the end and object of God's calling and election. For what could a holy God bestow in His benefits and beneficence other than holiness? Without holiness we could never be to the "praise of His glory." God's purpose in our calling and predestination is that we should be *holy*. Of course we could not enjoy a *standing* "before Him" if we were not in *state* holy and without blame, so how has all this come about? The answer is that our holiness is not inherent, but "in Him." We cannot go beyond what has been said before—"blessed with all spiritual blessings...in Christ." All that we are, we are in Christ.

Moule has here spoken in wisdom:

> The elect are to be viewed as *holy* and *spotless* because identified, for purposes of acceptance, with their absolutely Holy Head and Representative, "in Whom" they stand.*

---

*H. C. G. Moule, *Studies in Ephesians* (Grand Rapids: Kregel Publications, 1977), p. 46.

Our *state* is a result of "Christ in us," and our *standing* the result of our being "in Christ." As at the incarnation, God was in Christ and stood before us, so we are in Christ in His exaltation, and stand before God. God was manifest before us "in Christ" and we are manifest before Him in "Christ." We see God in Christ and God sees us in Christ. Christ is all there is of God before us, and Christ is all there is of us before God. We are accepted in the Beloved. We are before Him in Christ.

We see the Father in the Son and the Father sees us in the Son. We can only know and see each other in the Son. If we see the Father *we* look to Christ. If the Father sees us *He* looks to Christ. As we will never see God apart from Christ, so God will never see us apart from Christ. *O Christ, Thou art all to God and Thou art all to me!* Certainly fraternal relation with Christ is filial relation to God! It is "in Christ" we are holy and without blame before Him in love. Before Him! We, once shut out—the door closed and guarded by "flaming sword which turned every way."

But in the process of the unfolding program of redemption, the sword awoke against a man, saith Jehovah, "that is My fellow" (Zech. 13:7). It was the God-man. The Shepherd was smitten! The sword went to His heart to the hilt and by it the blood was shed which opened the way to God. Not to return to the presence of God in Adam, but to the presence of God in Christ.

We are holy and without blame before Him, in love, "in Christ," "in love"! Every demand of God's holiness for justice and judgment has been met in Christ's death and there is nothing for God to do but to lavish upon us the love the death of Christ let loose!

Not that God did not love us before Christ died, for Christ died because God loved us, but now that Christ has died, love finds its great medium of manifestation.

This brings us to the second statement.

2. "According to the good pleasure of His will" (v. 5)

As we have seen the result to the believer, this is the reason with God. "His will" is the cause and the consequence. That we, believers, have the position, place and privilege of a child is because the Father may thus bestow and bless as a result of Christ's redeeming work. Back of the will of God there is not a word. His will is the secret and the sequence of it all. "For," says the Apostle, "of Him, (origin) and through Him, (organ) and unto Him, (object) are all things" (Rom. 11:36).

There is but one standard of understanding and that is,— "according to the good pleasure of His will." There is but one measurement of such mercy and that is "according to the good pleasure of His will." When He predestinated us unto the "adoption of children," "through Jesus Christ" to "Himself," it was all "according to the good pleasure of His will." "The words *good pleasure* mean, deliberate beneficent resolve."*

—H. C. G. Moule.

He loved us and He adopts us for He wills it. For all this He has no assignable reason but "His will."

We would longer linger here where there is such love, but we must pass, for let it be remembered in the study of Ephesians, we are moving from "faith to faith" and from "glory to glory."

We'll now look at the third fact concerning His purpose in our predestination.

3. "To the praise of the glory of His grace" (v. 6)

Of this C. H. Spurgeon said:

> No truth is more plainly taught in God's Word than this; that the salvation of the sinner is entirely owing to the grace of God. Grace among the attributes is the Chrysostom, it has a golden mouth; it is Barnabas, it is full of consolation; it is Boanerges, for it thunders against self-righteousness. It is man's star of hope, the well-spring of His eternal life, and the seed of future bliss.

With a whole heart we may all with Spurgeon say, "Amen." But all definitions of grace now fail. Grace beggars defini-

*Ibid., p. 48.

tions. We may say "grace is the unmerited favor of God bestowed upon those who justly merited the judgment of God," but this too is not sufficient. There is only one satisfactory definition for "grace" and that is in Ephesians: "The riches of His grace in kindness toward us through Christ Jesus" (Eph. 2:7).

Grace in its proximate end is man's salvation. Says the Apostle, "The grace of God that bringeth salvation" (Titus 2:11).

> The primary truth is salvation by grace offered to man, but the ultimate is *God's own glory* and the manifestation of His moral excellence.
>
> —John Eadie.

The glory of grace is that merit does not help it nor demerit hinder it. It is no more hindered by sin than it is conditional upon works.

God is essentially and personally glorious. If there were no eyes to behold Him, no lips to praise Him, no creatures to obey Him, He would be infinitely glorious in Himself. He is the self-sufficient God and His reason for displaying and exhibiting His glory is for the benefit and blessing to His creatures.

Every attribute of God has its own glory, but when God glorifies His grace, He glorifies His whole character!

Omnipotence and goodness, justice and wisdom, infinitude and eternity, are essential attributes and have always been known and manifested. They did not need redemption to reveal them. *Grace comes to its revelation in redemption.* It is on the dark background of man's sin that grace comes to its manifold revelation.

One must concur with John Eadie:

> Grace with its characteristic glory, is a property in God's nature which never could have been displayed but for the introduction of sin, and God's design to save sinners (*Ephesians,* page 33).

We can now begin to understand somewhat of the words "to the praise of the glory of His grace." The greatness of grace is in that it displays every attribute of God. This thing which does the most for man does the most for God. When God glorifies His grace He glorifies His whole character.

If you want to behold justice at its greatest, look at the grace of God. If you want to see God's wisdom at its highest, look at the grace of God. If you want to see God's goodness in its ultimate, look at the grace of God. If you want to see God's mercy in highest manifestation, then look to the grace of God.

Grace exhibits in peculiar and particular splendor every attribute of God. Grace in redeeming man from his fallen nature reveals God in His glorious nature! The great God is encompassed in His grace! Grace is the platform upon which all the perfections of God are exhibited! We know God's omnipotence, skill, power and wisdom in the light of His grace. They are each bright enough in themselves, but, says Spurgeon, "They seem doubly bright in the brilliance of grace."

Think of it! God in saving man shows Himself! The cross was a great place of meeting. The cross is the one great "peace parliament" of the ages. It happened at the cross: the jarred attributes of God met together in harmony. Says the Psalmist:

Mercy and truth are met together; righteousness and peace have kissed each other (Ps. 85:10).

They could "meet together" and "kiss each other" at no other place but at the cross of Christ. They came to a great display here, for the cross was not only a place of meeting but a place of manifestation. Behold to what length the reconciling work of the cross extends!

The cross establishes truth and extends mercy; it provides righteousness and proclaims peace. Hallelujah, what a hill is Golgotha! It is *here the quarrelling quartet is satisfied* and reconciled. *Mercy* is glad that truth and justice is established and *truth* rejoices that mercy is manifested. *Righteousness* is exalted and exults that peace is preached and *peace* finds its tongue in righteousness revealed. Neither could get their demands or their deserts apart from the death of Christ.

And this is all "to the praise of the glory of His grace." When redemption is realized, then God will be glorified and man satisfied. Amen.

7

PREDESTINATION, REVELATION, DISPENSATION

Ephesians 1:5-10

He took us into favor in the Beloved One. As if God said, That the Beloved One is My Son, I must have them for sons, too. I must get them out of the mire to be before Me. A chain of things all in the heart of God, when the creature knew nothing about it.

—William Lincoln.

Predestination—"Having predestinated us unto," etc., (v. 5).

Revelation—"Having made known unto us the mystery of His will," etc., (v. 9).

Dispensation—"That in the dispensation of the fulness of times," etc., (v. 10).

Our God is the God of a goal. Man ignorantly, foolishly and flippantly sings, "I don't know where I'm going, but I'm on my way." With God there is no flippancy—majesty only. Known unto God are all His ways. This He knows from the beginning. He moves forward to a purposed point and a glorious goal. Predestination is but the vehicle of God's predetermination. God does because He is doing. Predestination implies also predesignation. There will be a termination of all God's predetermination. Man often fails to finish what he begins, but God never begins what He does not finish. This is to His glory and to ours also, for is it not written: "that He which hath begun a good work in you will perform it unto the day of Christ" (Phil. 1:6)?

In verse 5 we have the *Believer's Predestination.* This is the result of the "good pleasure of His will."

In verse 6 the *Believer's Acceptation,* for he is "accepted in the Beloved."

These are of the Godward side. But there is a "grace" side and in verse 7 we have the *Believer's Redemption,*—"in whom we have redemption through His Blood," and the measure of all this marvel and wonder is, "according to the riches of His grace." But the fruits of redemption lie buried in the roots of redemption. Redemption is threefold in its stages, viz., past, present and future. This Book of Ephesians calls attention to a "day of redemption" (1:14; 4:30). To grasp the intent of the Divine mind, a *Revelation* is required; and unquestionably John Eadie was right when he said, "The words 'wisdom' and 'prudence' are essentially connected with the disclosure of a mystery"—John Eadie on *Ephesians,* p. 43.

He prudently chooses the proper time. When Israel as a nation was yet in the "land," and the Gentiles as nations were looking to Israel for blessing; there would have been but little show of prudence to have made known the mystery of His will. When national Israel is set aside and Gentiles as nations, placed on the waiting list, awaiting the revival, return and restoration of Israel—then, and not till then—was the proper time for the revelation or, to "make known" "the mystery of His will." Herein is prudence.

"Wisdom and prudence" (vv. 8, 9) are also displayed in the method of disclosure. The "mysteries" of Ephesians were not committed to the prophets of the Old Testament. Says Paul, "How that *by revelation He made known unto me* the mystery" (Eph. 3:2).

Says Dr. Scofield in the *Scofield Reference Bible:*

The mystery hid in God was to make of Jew and Gentile a wholly new thing—the Church which is His (Christ's) Body. The revelation of this mystery was committed to Paul. In his writings alone we find the doctrine, position, walk and destiny of the Church.

Wisdom is often ascribed to God. Some boldly affirm that prudence cannot be predicated of God. But here is the word "prudence." The word "prudent" is used four times in the New Testament (Matt. 11:25; Luke 10:21; Acts 13: 7; 1 Cor. 1:19), but the word "prudence" but once and here. The Greek word *phronesis*—indicates thoughtfulness, goodness, practical wisdom, especially in the management of affairs. The word as used in the passage signifies that "practical sagacity which an initiator manifests in the disclosure of a mystery—a quality which, after the manner of men, is referred to God." But this word "mystery"—how mysterious! In fact, many teachers have made a great mystery of the "mystery." Inasmuch as we will often meet the word in Ephesians, it is well to come to some understanding of its biblical meaning early. The word has been used, misused and abused. Some are fearful and afraid; for through the medium of this word, much speculation and not a little false interpretation has been offered. The word as used here is *musterion.* It occurs in Ephesians six times as follows: 1:9; 3:3, 4, 9; 5:32; 6:19.

Handley G. Moule gives the proper definition of the word as follows:

> Always in the New Testament a truth undiscoverable except by revelation; never necessarily (as our popular use of the word may suggest) a thing unintelligible, or perplexing in itself.*

Indeed, the word "mystery" also carries the force of mystery only to the uninitiated. Here in Ephesians, we have the "mystery of His will" "*discoverable by revelation.*" There are a number of things in Scripture called "a mystery" which are undiscoverable apart from Divine revelation. Of these

---

*H. C. G. Moule, *Studies in Ephesians* (Grand Rapid: Kregel Publications, 1977), p. 50.

But now the passage under consideration is verse 10.

1. "That in the dispensation of the fulness of times" (v. 10a)

The word rendered "dispensation" is literally stewardship or house management. The word in the New Testament occurs in Luke 16:2, 3, 4, in the general sense of stewardship. *Oikonomia* is used with special reference to the Gospel and sometimes describes it as an arrangement or dispensation under charge of the Apostles or *stewards* (1 Cor. 4:1, 2; 9:17; Eph. 3:2; Col. 1:25; Titus 1:7; 1 Pet. 4:10). Dean Henry Alford said, "After a long and careful search, I am unable to find a word which will express the full meaning of *Oikonomia*." The mistake which has misled most commentators (except Stier) has been in taking it as a fixed *terminus a quo*—, the coming of Christ as in Galatians 4:4, whereas usage and sense determine it to mean the whole duration of the Gospel times. We believe this word speaks of both *duration* and *termination*. Jesus Christ is the dispenser or steward over the scheme of the ages. As the "firstborn" He stands as a responsible trustee unto God. In Him is the plan of the ages and in Him their prosecution and perfection also (Heb. 11:3). As House Manager or Administrator He has purpose and plan which moves on to perfection. He is putting the disordered house into order. It *marks God's time*, a time prearranged by Him and to which time all other "times" have been, under the administrative activity of the *Administrator of the ages*, moving on to this "full time dispensation."

God's Calendar is with Christ. It was the "fulness of time" when He came the first time (Gal. 4:4). It will be "times ness" when He comes again.

Let us remember that when Christ in Colossians is called "Firstborn of all creation" it is a step in His humiliation. first use of the title "firstborn" expresses its constant

things we hope to speak at other points in Ephesians. Pray, friends, do not make a mystery of the "mystery." It is a revealing, not a concealing. The "mystery" in Ephesians is expounded, not confounded.

The student doubtless has felt the trend and the tendency of these great truths. We have been constantly moving forward to a goal. Certainly swift currents in the counsel of God have been sweeping out toward a boundless sea. We shall soon reach the infinite bosom of the Divine objective. Having made mention of the Predestination, Redemption and Revelation we now come to *Dispensation*.

It is in verse 10, which is a summary of the "mystery of His will," that the colossal character of the Divine purpose breaks upon our vision. This purpose is expressed as a "dispensation of the fulness of times." We do not know all this verse means, nor do we think any have sounded its depths, much less exhausted its wealth of meaning.

8

CHRIST: CREATOR, CONSERVATOR AND CONSUMMATOR!

Ephesians 1:10-12

The universe was created to reach its perfection in Christ, and the eternal thought of God has been moving through countless ages of imperfection, development, pain and conflict, toward this great end. Crossed, resisted, defied, apparently thwarted by moral evil, the Divine purpose has been steadfast, has never been surrendered. Its energy has been wonderfully revealed in the incarnation and death of the Lord Jesus Christ. Its final triumph is secure.

—R. W. Dale of Birmingham.

CHRIST IS THE Divine goal! To Him all things move as by Him "all things were made!" He is not only Creator but Conservator and Consummator! He is the Alpha and also the Omega. He is the beginning and the end. Here is the title of all titles. The Lord Jesus Christ A.Z., The Alpha and Omega, the First and the Last, and all that the alphabet may spell out between.

Surely John Robertson was right when speaking of Christ in the Scriptures, he said: "He is revealed by this revelation, the center and the circumference of the 66."

In Him is the centralization of creation and revelation. The created works of God and the revealed Word of God are both Christo-centric. In Him is originality, instrumentality, centrality and finality.

Those things which were made by Him in *creation* are now held by Him in *conservation* and in time fullness will be brought by Him to Divine *consummation*. He is the Governor directing all things to the goal. Jesus Christ is in charge of the universe. "He is before all things" refers to position in person and power, as well as to priority in plan and time. There is a forward movement in all of the Scriptures. There is no going back to Christ, but going *on to Christ*. There is progress in the plan of God. God trusted in Christ before He asked any of His creatures to do so. He imposed upon Him and invested wi[th] Him His eternal purpose.

The Eternal Word is, therefore, the *goal* of the univers[e]. He was the *starting point*. Things must end in unity as [they] proceeded in unity, and the center of this unity is Christ. Scriptures open with "In the beginning God." They w[ill end] with "God" (1 Cor. 15:28).

This is the subject of which Ephesians 1:10 is the su[m].

That in the dispensation of the fulness of times He mig[ht gather] together in one, all things in Christ, both which are in he[aven,] which are on earth; even in Him (Eph. 1:10).

It is Christ **Consummator!**

As we write we are not unmindful of much th[at is] today in a "show of wisdom" and must say once [again that] the "summing up of all things in Christ" doe[s not give us] explicit information in regard to the destiny of [men in] eternity. This remains in Christ's hands (John [   ). But] we have never found any way to logically, et[ymologically, or] theologically make the word "things" to mea[n "men." We] are slow to yield our New Testament to [the modern] versions. We believe that much that is [offered is] perversion. We are not willing to receive [a new] Testament from the Greek at the han[ds of men] attempting to "arrive at the text" let us [beware lest we] receive a "pretext." Some think it a hig[h thing to say] "the Greek says so-and-so,"—but it [may be used to] cover a multitude of ignorance rather [than to reveal] wisdom.

Reuben, thou art my first born, *my might,* and the beginning of *my strength,* the *excellency of dignity,* and the *excellency of power* (Gen. 49:3).

As the "firstborn," Christ became responsible for the household and the children of the household. This was the dignity and power conferred on the "firstborn." One of these days Christ will render an account of His stewardship as the "firstborn" and not only "in the dispensation of the fulness of times," to bring to order the disordered house, but triumphantly shout, "Here I am, Father and all the children Thou hast given Me" (Heb. 2:13; see Is. 8:17). First-born refers to His *position* and not His person as Russellism would seek to teach, thus reviving the Gnosticism of the first centuries. The Arians also endeavored to draw from this verse the inference that the Son was a created being, that He was the first-born of every creature.

The word "firstborn" is not a reference to His Person, but to His *position* and *priority* as related to creation.

O that men would learn to distinguish between the Person of Christ and the Position of Christ.

O that men would learn to distinguish between who He was and what He did.

"Firstborn" is not who He was, but *what He did.* Christ was always who He is. He changed position but Person never!

Christ is not a creature, but a **Creator.** He is the Head of God's household. He assumed it as the "firstborn." He stands at the head of all creation. He is the Administrator of affairs, and, as such Administrator, He will sum up the disorder of both spheres, for, that

2. "He might gather together in one, all things in Christ, both which are in heaven and which are on earth; even in Him" (v. 10b)

or in the words of the *Weymouth* translation:*

---

*Richard F. Weymouth, *New Testament in Modern Speech* (Grand Rapids: Kregel Publications, 1978), p. 515.

And this is in harmony with God's merciful purpose for the government of the world when the times are ripe for it—the purpose which He has cherished in His own mind of restoring the whole creation to find its one Head in Christ; yes, things in Heaven and things on earth, to find their one Head in Him.

Now we understand Stewardship and are introduced to the Summary and the Spheres.

Stewardship "that in the dispensation of the fulness of times."

Summary "gather together in one all things in Christ."

Spheres "both which are in heaven and in earth."

Moule is right in saying, "The Greek may be literally represented by, 'that He might *head up* all things in Christ.' "* The verb is only used elsewhere in Romans 13:9, where the Authorized Version reads, "it is briefly comprehended"— summed up. Therefore let us so read—"To sum up all things in Christ as Head."

"Gather together" implies a scattering. He gathers only the things scattered. Things scattered implies *disorder*. This statement therefore indicates that Christ will *put in order* the things in disorder. He will restore things to their primal unity. The discord and disorder will under Him resolve into eternal harmony. In Colossians we have *unity in origin* with Christ as its *Author*. In Ephesians we have *unity in the ultimate* with Christ as its *Finisher*.

Sin is the cause of this disorder. Sin is the separator and scatterer! Sin separated and scattered things in both spheres,—"in heaven and on earth." At the opening verses of the Bible we are introduced to these two spheres: "In the beginning God created the heavens and the earth" (R.V.). These two spheres have been invaded by sin and of course the original sinner in the universe of God is Satan. Jesus Christ "will destroy the works of the devil."

The phrase "things in heaven" denotes the higher and

---

*H. C. G. Moule, *Studies in Ephesians* (Grand Rapids: Kregel Publications, 1977), p. 57.

more distant spheres of creation. These along with things on the earth are to be placed in the dispensation of times fullness under the One Headship of Christ.

Sin—Spheres—Scattered

Sin has invaded and uprooted the harmony of the universe.
—Marcus Rainsford.

Rebellion produced disorder, the unity of the kingdom was broken, earth was morally severed from heaven.
—John Eadie.

Sin has scattered and separated things in heaven and in earth.

1. Sin Separated God and His Creatures
This especially refers to created intelligences, angels and creatures of His creation. How sin has invaded their ranks! Some are in chains of darkness, imprisoned, awaiting judgment and eternal destiny (2 Pet. 2:4; Jude 1:6). A faithful company stand before His face—performing His will (Heb. 1:14). These remain unmoved by rebellion and apostasy.

2. Sinful Man and a Holy God were Separated
(Is. 59:2, cf. Rev. 7:15; 21:3)

3. Men and Angels were Separated
This shall not always be so (John 1:51)

4. Nations were Separated from Nations
(Gen. 11)

5. Jews Separated from Gentiles
(Gen. 12)

6. Death—Dissolution Separated Body, Soul and Spirit
(1 Thess. 5:23)

7. Israel Was Scattered among the Nations

Thus we see the task laid upon Christ. Ephesians celebrates

the triumph in Christ. The death of Christ is the means to this end. His mediative work has secured it.

As a stone dropped in a lake creates those widening and concentric circles, which ultimately reach the furthest shores, so the deed done on Calvary has sent its blessed undulations through the distant spheres and realms of God's great empire. Redemption *through His Blood!* The Headship of Christ is the hope of the Universe. Hallelujah!

He will "gather together," "sum up" all things in "Himself." "Himself" is the ultimate and the final.

This "summing up" has been likened to the reunion of a dispersed army.

Again it has been presented as the addition of arithmetical sums. This general idea of summation is correct, with the additional thought of recollection. Christ will collect again things under one Head. O what a collection!

The words of John Eadie, a man mighty in the Scriptures, are wise and well may they be here appended:

> Since the days of Origen, the advocates of the doctrine of universal restoration have sought a proof-text in this passage. The context, however, plainly limits the "things on earth" to such as have redemption by His Blood. Unredeemed man is ignored. But the punishment of the impenitent affects not the unity of Christ's government. Evil has lost its power of creating disorder, for it is punished, confined, and held as a very feeble thing in the grasp of the Almighty Avenger.

Thus we are left gazing upon Jesus Christ, the Son of God, the Creator, the Conservator, and the Consummator—left looking upon Him, in whose dispensation or stewardship, all things are to be gathered up, so that, of the present fragments scattered about in two spheres, "nothing shall remain." *My Jesus, I love Thee! Amen.*

9

THE SEALING AND SECURING SPIRIT

Ephesians 1:13-14

Oh, how precious must we be to God, who has not only given us His Son to die for our sins and redeemed us to an inheritance predestined for us, but has also made us in Him an inheritance and possession for Himself, sealing us unto the day of redemption.
—Marcus Rainsford.

WE HAVE FOUND ourselves to be the object of the eternal purpose of God the *Father,* and through Redemption, the present possession of the *Son,* but now we are to hear of Him who as yet has not been mentioned—the *Holy Spirit*—the third person of the ever blessed and adorable trinity!

That which was *essentially* ours by the will of God the Father and *instrumentally* ours by the Blood of the Son is now *experimentally* ours in the Holy Spirit.

In whom ye also trusted, after that ye heard the Word of Truth, the Gospel of your salvation: in whom also after ye believed, ye were sealed with that Holy Spirit of promise, which is the earnest of our inheritance until the redemption of the purchased possession, unto the praise of His glory (Eph. 1:13, 14).

A brief analysis of the verses under consideration may help the student to better grasp the sum and substance of our present chapter.

1. The Place of Sealing,—"in Christ" "in Whom"

2. The Person Sealing,—"that Holy Spirit of promise"

3. The Persons Sealed,—"in whom ye were sealed"

4. The Purpose of Sealing,—"earnest of our inheritance"

5. The Property Sealed,—"the purchased possession"

6. The Pledge of Sealing,—"unto the day of redemption"

7. The Praise of Sealing,—"His glory"

Divine Declaration of Purchase

Let us now consider this Divine declaration of purchase! Here the Divine Father by publication gives notification of a purchased possession!

Let men, angels and devils take notice and keep off His possessions! The Church is His claim and herein is the Declaration of Purchase with purpose and promise attached! This, beloved believer, is the "Gospel of your salvation," the Word ye "believed and received." A Salvation which not only made you *safe* from the penalty of judgment which, in the past, should have justly fallen, but a Salvation which *secures* you for the future by means of the Spirit's Seal. To Him be praise!

And, oh, the holy harmony of the glorious Godhead, for what the *Father* decrees the *Son* accomplishes, and to the work of the Son the *Holy Spirit* sets His seal! As John set his seal to the Word of God (John 5:33) the Holy Spirit set His seal to the work of Christ. The sealing of the believer is the Spirit's Amen to the work of Christ. The Spirit indeed "answers to the Blood."

Again, what a seal is this—for it is a loving seal—the Holy Spirit Himself! Behold the interlinking chain of Divine security,—the *Sealer* is God, the believer is the possession *sealed*, the Spirit is the *Seal* and the place wherein the believer is by God sealed by the Holy Spirit, the Seal, is "in Christ." But of this we shall see more as we continue; now we'll consider the Sealer, the Seal and the Sealed.

The first mention in the New Testament of the Father's sealing is not in Ephesians, nor is it the sealing of the believer in Christ. In John 6:27 we read: "Labor not for the meat which perisheth, but for that meat which endureth unto everlasting life, which the Son of man shall give unto you: *for him hath God the Father sealed.*" In John, the Father seals the *Son.* In Ephesians He seals the *Sons.* In this experience the believer is as his Lord.

Dr. A. J. Gordon has spoken significantly of the sealing of the Son on this wise:

> This sealing must evidently refer back to His reception of the Spirit at the Jordan. One of the most instructive writers on the Hebrew worship and ritual tells us that it was the custom for the priest to whom the service pertained, having selected a lamb from the flock, to inspect it with the most minute scrutiny, in order to discover if it was without physical defect, and then to seal it with the Temple seal, thus certifying that it was fit for sacrifice and for food. Behold the Lamb of God presenting Himself for inspection at the Jordan! Under the Father's omniscient scrutiny He is found to be "a Lamb without blemish and without spot." From the opening heaven God gives witness to the fact in the words, "This is My beloved Son in whom I am well pleased," and then He puts the Holy Ghost upon Him, the testimony to His Sonship, the seal of His separation unto sacrifice and service.

Spiritual Significance of the Spirit's Sealing

1. A Seal Is for Preservation

"Preserved in Jesus Christ" (Jude 1:1). Shut up by God in Christ and sealed in Him by the Holy Spirit. Once "dead in trespasses and sins," *now in Christ* where we cannot get out or none can get in to take us out. *What a position beyond all opposition!* Safety and certainty, secured by the Spirit who seals us in the Son.

The act of preserving is a simple transaction. The housewife receives the fruit of the season and preserves it in the receptacle provided, carefully sealing it within from and beyond the reach of hostile elements, which would contribute to its fermentation and corruption. Preserved and sealed, the fruit is held in store for the day of feasting, when friends will gather about the table, or a time of need beyond a season of fruit.

The believer, the fruit of Christ's passion, is preserved in Christ and sealed within Christ by the Holy Spirit, unto a future day—the day of redemption. No, we trust but little or none in the "perseverance of the Saints," we trust wholly and altogether in the preserving and sealing of the saints by the Holy Spirit of God, who, when once a believer is *in Christ, seals him in!* Oh, the keeping and preserving power of the Holy Spirit, the Sealer of the Saints in Christ! Kept from the corruption of the present age! Kept from the evil power of the present age! Kept from the evil person who rules the present age and directs its energies! Praise to Him "who hath delivered us from this present evil age, according to the will of God the Father" (Gal. 1:4).

2. A Seal Signifies Authentication

Whom Christ saves the Holy Spirit seals. The Holy Spirit honors the "Blood." Where Christ has made atonement the Holy Spirit vouchsafes anointment. The Holy Spirit seals and secures those for whom Christ suffered. The Holy Spirit sets His seal that the work of Christ is satisfactory.

Again, behold the holy harmony of the glorious God-head—God the Father acknowledges and bears witness to the finished work of Christ by raising Him from the dead—the Holy Spirit bears witness to the finished work of Christ by raising Him from the dead—the Holy Spirit bears witness to the finished work of Christ by sealing those whom Christ has quickened from the dead.

Note how Ridout explains it:

> A beautiful illustration of this occurs in the Levitical ordinances of the Old Testament. In the consecration of the priests and in the restoration of the leper, the blood of sacrifice was put upon ear and hand and foot, marking the whole man as redeemed (Lev. 8:23; 14:14). After this application of the blood they were sprinkled with oil, a type of the Spirit. Particularly in the case of the leper, we are told that the oil was put upon ear and hand and foot, *upon the blood.* So the Spirit of God seals us because of the Blood, the work of Christ. It is not a matter of personal

worthiness or of personal faithfulness, but of the value of the work of Christ. Have we rested in that? Then we are sealed, Divinely authenticated as belonging to God by His Spirit.

The Holy Spirit's one delight is in attestation and confirmation of the work of Christ! Where Christ has shed His Blood, the Spirit sets His seal! God be glorious in our eyes!!

3. A Seal Is to Prevent Molestation

Let none tamper with the seal God has set. We have a salvation which is beyond molestation and the Spirit's seal signifies the same. The colossal lie of the first century was a conclusive testimony to the fixed truth of all centuries: "Christ died for our sins ... was buried ... and rose again the third day" (1 Cor. 15:3).

When Christ was laid away in the tomb He was sealed then by the Roman Government. This was done at the instigation of the Chief Priests and Pharisees, for they said unto Pilate:

> Sir, we remember that that deceiver said, while He was yet alive, After three days I will rise again. Command therefore that the sepulchre be made sure until the third day, lest His disciples come by night, and steal Him away, and say unto the people, He is risen from the dead: so the last error shall be worse than the first (Matt. 27:63, 64).

The answer of Pilate was, "Ye have a watch: go your way, make it as sure as ye can" (Matt. 27:65).

It was a Roman seal, placed by Roman soldiers under the governor's direction—who would dare molest? The seal was to prevent molestation, and mark you, no human fingers ever touched the seal that sealed Christ within Joseph's tomb. There was not one in the land who had the daring to defy human law and touch an affixed seal.

If, as the colossal lie concocted in the dilemma of the priests and Pharisees, the disciples came and "stole Him away while they slept" in order that they might circulate a resurrection story and thus by their lie confirm this lie of Him who had said, "on the third day He would arise from the dead;" why, we ask, were the disciples not brought to judgment, for they remained several months in and about Jerusalem and were in easy reach of the law and deserved its full penalty for such an atrocious crime as removing a seal which was by Roman law affixed?

Why were not the soldiers who slept at the post of duty while this ghoulish thieving was going on and this stupendous fraud was being enacted, why, we say, were they not punished? For Roman law provided punishment as a penalty. And why was not the captain of the guard punished for failure to patrol his guards; for if he had been doing his duty, he would have come suddenly upon the sleepers and would have taken their garments and presented them at the tribunal the following day as a witness against the sleepers, for unquestionably this is the meaning and significance of "blessed is he that keepeth his garments" (Rev. 16:15).

That seal was placed on that tomb to prevent molestation, and no human finger fumbled at that seal. No human feet passed those watchers. It was an *earthquake* from beneath, and the *angel* of the Lord from heaven, that removed that seal and rolled away the stone. It was the Lord of Life who got up and majestically walked out. The Roman government has no case against the Son of God, and for this reason the case was dropped and resolved into a lie.

The Holy Spirit's seal is also to prevent molestation. Let none touch or tamper where the Holy Spirit has set His seal. None can pass this Holy watcher and steal believers from Christ. The Holy Spirit has sealed us up in Christ beyond molestation. We are "in Christ" and Christ is in heaven at the right hand of God. None can molest us unless they may wrest us from Him. The *believer's position in Christ is as secure as Christ Himself* on the throne of God. Until He is deposed, can we be molested? Never. Strong words these. Yes, but not so strong as He!

4. A Seal Secures in Tribulation

The drama of the Day of the Lord is ready for enactment. The great day has come! But upon the earth these judgments cannot fall until a remnant from the twelve tribes of Israel are sealed and thus secured. The remnant of the nation must stand for the rest of the nation. This is as it has ever been. Therefore we read:

> And after these things I saw four angels standing on the four corners of the earth, holding the four winds of the earth, that the wind should not blow on the earth, nor on the sea, nor on any tree. And I saw another angel ascending from the east, having the seal of the Living God: and he cried with a loud voice to the four angels, to whom it was given to hurt the earth and the sea, Saying, "Hurt not the earth, neither the sea, nor the trees, till we have sealed the servants of our God in their foreheads" (Rev. 7:1-3).

Then follows the sealing. "One hundred and forty and four thousand of all the tribes of the children of Israel."

Unlike the Church, which escapes the tribulation, the twelve tribes of Israel are sealed to pass through the tribulation. A seal stands for security in tribulation, whether it be the tribulation period or any tribulation present. There are many things which would separate us, and among them and first is "tribulation" (see Rom. 8:35), but *our security in Christ is our sufficiency* for these things. We are sealed in Him, for though tribulation may come, it cannot separate. Whom God has sealed none and nothing can separate.

5. A Seal Signifies Identification

Having given notification by proclamation and publication of the purchase of a possession, God also stamps and seals the believer for future identification. "The Lord knows them that are His." "This seal is on the very foundation of God" (2 Tim. 2:19). Whoever they be and whoever they are, He knows them and they are sealed for identification. "I am the Good Shepherd, and know My sheep" (John 10:14).

This seal cannot be effaced. Time cannot do it. Trial cannot do it. Testing or tribulation cannot efface, deface or obscure this identifying seal. Death, dissolution or decay cannot do it. Mortality cannot swallow it up or the grave erase the Divine engraving! It remains affixed through all changes. This seal is

beyond the tampering of time and the plundering of the
elements. Sealed with the Holy Spirit of promise. Never
beyond His recognition. Says Edward H. Bickersteth:

> The allusion to the seal as a pledge of purchase would be
> peculiarly intelligible to the Ephesians, for Ephesus was a
> maritime city, and an exclusive trade in timber was carried on
> there by the shipmasters of the neighboring ports. The method of
> purchase was this: The merchant, after selecting his timber,
> stamped it with his own signet, which was an acknowledged sign
> of ownership. He often did not carry off his possession at the
> time; it was left in the harbor with other floats of timber; but it
> was chosen, bought, and stamped; and in due time the merchant
> sent a trusty agent with the signet, who, finding that timber which
> bore a corresponding impress, claimed and brought it away for
> the master's use. Thus the Holy Spirit impresses on the soul now
> the image of Jesus Christ; and this is the sure pledge of the
> everlasting inheritance.*

Thus the *believer is stamped and sealed* for identification.
The faithful Agent has done His work and has done it well.
The Lord will get His own from among the dead at the
appointed time. They are sealed for identification unto the
day of redemption. None of them will be lost who are in His
love. His seal is our security.

An announcement was made from a public platform: A
purse containing considerable money and other valuables has
been found. It will be returned to the owner upon proper
identification. Soon a lady approached declaring she was the
owner. Said she, "There was $20.00 in gold, also some
currency, a signet ring and a watch within the purse, which
was black pin seal, lined with dark blue satin and on one side
were monogram initials A.G.W." Said the Moderator, "You
have accurately and properly identified the property, it is
yours." God knows His property without and within and will

*Edward H. Bickersteth, *The Holy Spirit: His Person and Work* (Grand
Rapids: Kregel Publications, 1959), p. 176.

claim His own at the day of redemption and has stamped each one with the seal of identification.

6. A Seal Is for Destination

We are sealed with the Holy Spirit of promise "unto the day of redemption" (Eph. 4:30).

In 1:14 the "Holy Spirit" is the "earnest of our inheritance *until* the redemption of the purchased possession." In Ephesians 4:30 the Holy Spirit has sealed us *unto* the day of redemption. "Until" and "unto" are not synonymous. Often one hears Revelation 2:10 misquoted as follows: "Be thou faithful *until* death and I will give thee a crown of life." The word is *unto*. There is a difference with a Divine distinction. "Until" speaks of incompleteness. "Unto" speaks of completion. "Until" speaks of arrest, "unto" of arrival. "Until" signifies the "continuance" of an action up to the time of another action. "Unto" places the limit and implies termination. "Unto" speaks of "destination."

We are sealed by the Holy Spirit "unto" the day of redemption, implying *destination.* There is to be a "day of redemption." Redemption is not fully understood and often misunderstood. Many think of "redemption" as a fact accomplished in the past. The *roots* of redemption lie in the past, but the *fruits* of redemption are future. The tenses of Christ's redeeming triumph are significantly stated in Second Corinthians 1:10, "Who delivered us from so great a death (past work of Christ), and doth deliver: (present work of Christ) in whom we trust that He will yet deliver us" (Christ's future work). At the Cross redemption's purchased price was paid. At the Second Coming of Christ, "the redemption of the purchased possession." It is unto this time, the Holy Spirit has sealed and secured us. Unto the Holy Spirit is committed our survival and arrival unto this day.

At the time we are writing, all Europe is covered with war clouds—dark and ominous. Perils on land and sea await this part of the world for which it seems a baptism of blood is due. We have just read the following:

> The British fleet sailed under sealed orders today. No hint of its destination has been given. It is believed to be a movement intended to mystify all foreign powers and prevent any probability of an airplane attack on the dreadnought squadron.

Certainly we take no pleasure in this note of devilish and dreadful war, but it illustrates our consideration that *a seal is for destination.* The British fleet sailed under sealed orders, no hint of *destination* is given.

The Church, the Body of Christ, believers of this hostile time present, is under sealed orders. Sealed by the Holy Spirit—but point of destination is fully known and already revealed before the time. "Sealed unto the day of redemption." This is our destination. No mystery movements, no fear of enemies or failure. No—but "unto the day of redemption."

7. A Seal Is for Presentation

The "day of redemption" will be a day of *presentation.* In the exchange of gifts among sovereigns, the gifts are sealed for presentation. Among us all in the exchange of gifts at the holiday season, there is a custom of wrapping carefully and sealing the gifts for presentation. The gifts must be delivered with marks of love and care, which make for preparation in presentation. A package carelessly wrapped, in a wrinkled, crumpled manner, would speak of relieving an obligation rather than bestowing a gift of affection.

When Christ presents His Church, which has been sealed by the Holy Spirit, it will be a "glorious Church, not having spot or wrinkle or any such thing."

Who have not, in the height of a holiday season, been the recipients of a package carefully arranged and marked with a seal, "Do Not Open till Christmas"? The joy would come in the morning! That which was sealed in secret would then be displayed openly. The seals would be broken, and eyes would feast on the love token. O the joy of the morning! There is a day of presentation. The believer is sealed for the day. Therefore in benediction, let us sing,

Now unto Him that is able to keep you from falling, and to present you faultless before the presence of His glory with exceeding joy, to the only wise God our Savior, be glory and majesty, dominion and power, both now and ever. Amen (Jude 1:24, 25).

10

PAUL'S FIRST PRAYER
The Three "Whats"

Ephesians 1:17-23

If prayer for others is a barometer of our own spiritual life, we can realize what Saint Paul felt was necessary for himself by his prayers for others.

In Ephesians there are two petitions, and nothing fuller and deeper is found in any of the apostle's writings. This Epistle represents the high water mark of Christian privilege and possibility.

—W. H. Griffith Thomas, D.D.
in *The Prayers of Saint Paul.*

WE HAVE NOW arrived at the first prayer of the Apostle Paul in the Ephesian letter and are to hear the Apostle pray! It is reported that students of the saintly Bengel secreted themselves within the draperies of his bedroom that they might hear his retiring prayer. John A. Bengel, author of *The New Testament Commentary* (Kregel Publications, 1971), knelt before God, and this is what and all that he said:

I thank Thee, Lord Jesus, that we are on the same old terms. Good-night. Amen.

To think we are permitted to hear the Apostle Paul pray! And what a prayer—a prayer uttered by the Holy Spirit through him! A prayer of spiritual revelation to have permanent place on the pages of Divine Inspiration!

Hearken! he prays:

That the God of our Lord Jesus Christ, the Father of glory, may give unto you the spirit of wisdom and revelation in the knowledge of Him: the eyes of your understanding being enlightened; that ye may know what is the hope of His calling, and what the riches of the glory of His inheritance in the saints, and what is the exceeding greatness of His power toward us who believe, according to the working of His mighty power, which He wrought in Christ, when He raised Him from the dead, and set Him at His own right hand in the heavenly places, far above all principality, and power, and might, and dominion, and every name that is named, not only in this world, but also in that which is to come: and hath put all things under His feet, and gave Him to be the Head over all things to the Church, which is His Body, the fulness of Him that filleth all in all (Eph. 1:17-23).

Let us prayerfully meditate upon this prayer, concerning which Bishop Moule has so pertinently remarked, "The prayer that the saints may fully realize their Divine privileges and prospects in Christ."*

It is addressed (1:17) to the "God of our Lord Jesus Christ, the Father of glory."

This statement has startled many. Some think the statement infers the Son to be secondary Deity. Such is not the case. We must remember that the person of Christ has never changed. He is who He was and will always be who He is. "Thou changest not." *He has never changed in Person,* He is as immutable as God Himself who indeed He is.

Position Changed, Person the Same

He has, however, changed in position. The only thing He can change is His position, but His person never. He has been manifested under various names, but His nature has never changed. The same in nature is He yesterday, today and forever. He cannot in person and nature be other than He was and is and will be. He is as immutable as He is infallible.

---

*H. C. G. Moule, *Studies in Ephesians* (Grand Rapids: Kregel Publications, 1977), p. 55.

Indeed the latter is the result of the former. Not only is the Son of the same essence with the Father, but He is God in and from Himself.

The incarnation did not in the least alter the nature and person of the Lord. At the incarnation He changed His position and manifestation, but in person He was who He always was, but now (though incarnate) He was still God, but *God manifested in the flesh.*

The Father is the God of the *Son incarnate* in a sense which the incarnation imposed on Him—not by any change of His nature. Never as long as God gives us a pen with which to write or a pulpit from which to preach, shall we ever preach Christ to be less than He is, for *He is God.* Yes, indeed, there is a vast difference and distance between the Christ of Divine revelation and human reason!

The "Father of glory" is also a unique phrase and unlike any other. Whatever may be the radiation and emanation of glory is due to its origination. The universe has had much display of God's glory and in the future the exhibition of His glory will surpass any display that has been made in times past. "The whole earth" is to be filled with "His glory" (Is. 6:3). But God is here called the "Father of glory," the One in whom glory had parenthood. Glory is the offspring of God. Without God there would be no glory, for He is the "Lord of glory" (1 Cor. 2:8) and the "God of glory" (Ps. 29:3).

But we believe the glory, to which Paul refers in the address of his prayer, is not so much the essential glory which in God doth dwell, but that glory which He has won for Himself as the "God of our Lord Jesus Christ," for the Lord Jesus Christ is the glory of God. The glory of which God is possessed has no medium of manifestation apart from the Lord Jesus Christ, who is the sole exhibitor of His glory. God is the Father of this glory, which glory is on exhibition in and through the Son. It is in the face of Jesus Christ we behold the glory of God. Christ is God's glory and God's glory is Christ.

Then follows the Apostle's petition that God would give unto the believer "the spirit of wisdom and revelation in the knowledge of Him" (Eph. 1:17). We have seen in former studies how the believer is secured by the Spirit as an Earnest and Seal, but now the Apostle's imploring prayer is that the Holy Spirit give "wisdom and revelation."

William Tyndale translates it:

> That He might give to you the spirit of wisdom and open to you the knowledge of Himself.

This is a wisdom which infinitely transcends human intelligence and a revelation which lies far beyond the searching of human science. It is wisdom and revelation which lies wholly within the bestowal of the Holy Spirit. There are things which flesh and blood cannot reveal unto us. These things are the things of the Spirit of God and the Spirit of God delights in imparting "knowledge of Him."

Human philosophy may be summed up in a well-known axiom, "know thyself," but the Christian's faith rises to concern far above things "under the sun" and has for its axiom, "know God."

It is not the acknowledgment of God of which we are now speaking, but the *knowledge of God.* To know God we must have the Holy Spirit of wisdom and revelation. Sin has closed our eyes, clouded our minds, clogged our vision and stultified our affections, and no human power can deliver us from this sin and Satan-imposed bondage and burden. If we are ever again to see or to know, the eyes of our understanding must be opened by God, the Holy Spirit. How absolute is our dependence upon God. When will we cease from man and supplicate a Sovereign Spirit God?

The "Three Whats"

1. "What is the hope of His calling?" (v. 18)
2. "What is the riches of the glory of His inheritance in the saints?" (v. 18)
3. "What is the exceeding greatness of His power to usward who believe?" (v. 19)

The prayer turns upon this pivot. The "three whats" give

unto it its subject and scope. It is for the comprehension of those "three whats" the Apostle has prayed for us all.

Before we further proceed let each reader with the writer bow in the presence of Him who is the Lord and pray for enlightened understanding and opened eyes. Everything here depends upon Spirit-opened eyes. The scene may be fair, the light may be bright, and glorious the vision may be; but if the sight be gone, all is vain.

C. H. Spurgeon wrote:

> Zedekiah had his eyes put out by the King of Babylon, and then he was taken down to the imperial city, but for what he could enjoy of all its splendor he might as well have been in a desert. There were vast halls and palaces, and hanging gardens, and a city wall which was the wonder of the world, so that Babylon is called by the prophet, "The glory of kingdoms and the beauty of the Chaldees' excellency," but the blinded monarch beheld nothing of all the grandeur of the golden city, and to him her wealth was as though it had not been.

So with the believer, he can know nothing nor see anything of these "three whats" until the Holy Spirit, the Divine Oculist, has operated upon the vision.

"What is the hope of His calling?"

"What the riches of the glory of His inheritance in the saints?"

"What is the exceeding greatness of His power?"

1. The First "What"

"What is the hope of His calling?"

Paul prays that the believers' eyes may be opened to know "what is the hope of His calling," that is, the calling of the Church, the object of God's special dealing in the present dispensation, and the subject of the Epistle to the Ephesians.

Each calling of God bears with it a "hope" which is in perfect harmony with the "calling." God never confuses. He never issues a heavenly call with an earthly hope, nor an earthly call with a heavenly hope, and in this regard the callings of God are without repentance.

The call of God was sent to Israel. National Israel was called in Abraham and confirmed to him and his seed in covenants. The purpose of Jehovah's call to Israel was for the "blessing of the families of the earth." This will be readily seen by a reference to Genesis 12:1-3; 15:4-21; 17:1-9; 22:15-18.

This calling and covenant made with Abraham was confirmed unto Isaac (Gen. 26:1-5) and in turn confirmed also unto Jacob (Gen. 28:3, 4, 13-15). It was continued through the chosen line of Israel and did not suffer annulment at the coming of Christ, for we read, "Now I say that Jesus Christ was a minister of the circumcision for the truth of God to *confirm the promises* made unto the fathers" (Rom. 15:8).

The covenant of God stands sure and while as yet the nations of the earth have not realized the fullness of the blessings promised through Israel, nevertheless, the Word of God standeth sure and our God is a covenant-keeping God. "He keepeth His covenant unto generations and generations."

The *hope of Israel's calling* is the earth. In the earth God gave them a Land, a City, a House and a Throne and for these, unto this day, Israel has hope. This is the hope of Israel's calling and this hope shall be realized. No student of the Bible will read Isaiah 61:3 to 62:1 without assurance that their *state* shall ultimately harmonize with their *calling*.

The *Gentiles* or nations of the earth have also a "calling" and a "hope." God has called them through Israel, and let it be remembered that while God dwells in the tents of Shem (Israel), yet "God shall enlarge Japheth" and Japheth shall dwell under the booth and the blessing of Shem. The Gentiles as nations are yet to enjoy, in the purpose of God, great national blessing, but this blessing is to be brought to them through Israel, the Divine channel.

O that it were ours at this time to collect and collate the future glory of the nations of the earth as revealed in the Scriptures. They shall not always be in a state of war, but their future attitude is one of the *worship of Christ,* the *King of all the kings* and the *Lord of all the lords.*

The Church is also called and unto the *Church* is also given a *"hope"* which is in holy harmony with the "calling." The Church is called "into the heavenlies." It is the place of her present standing (Eph. 1:3), her present strife (Eph. 6:12) and her future service (Eph. 3:10). Her wealth is in the heavenlies; her warfare is there and her walk should be of that character.

It is indeed sad to record that the church has forgotten the primitive hope and with the loss of this hope has also suffered the loss of primitive faith and love. Eyes that should be lifted to the heavenlies are now fixed upon the earth. Instead of looking to her spiritual sphere, the church is now taken up with Social Service. What was once done in His name is now done in humanity's name. When the church failed in Christian compassion she fell to social service. The church is bent to a world task which is entirely self-imposed. The church is now busy blowing out the red light, cleaning up the slums, reforming politics, controlling government, conducting civic affairs, making the slate and breaking the slate at the primaries! The ballot box has taken the place of the Bible.

If the church of God would preach the Gospel with as much fervor and faithfulness as it enters into reformation, true light would, through the regeneration of the sinner, be introduced into this world's present darkness.

"O how the mighty are fallen!" The *church* has forgotten that her *one attitude is to look for her Lord from heaven.* The modern emphasis is a distortion of the Apostle's plain declaration. Much modern preaching proclaims that our citizenship is of this world. Paul claims that "our citizenship is in heaven; from whence also we look for the Savior, the Lord Jesus Christ" (Phil. 3:20). We stand with the Apostle Paul, not with the present apostasy. Our eyes have been opened in answer to the Apostle's prayer. We have no human intuition, but we have received Divine illumination.

2. The Second "What"

"What is the riches of the glory of His inheritance in the saints?"

That we have an inheritance in Him is often the subject of

our meditation and the cause of much exultation! We well know that "He is the Heir of all things" (Heb. 1:2) and that we are joint-heirs with Him, but here, (O the marvel of it!) the Apostle desires our eyes to be opened to know what an inheritance He has *in His saints.*

Dr. W. H. Griffith Thomas calls attention to the fact that "we must never forget that the biblical ideas as associated with 'heir' and 'inheritance' always refer to possession, and not, as in ordinary phraseology to succession."

The saints have a wonderful inheritance in their Savior, but can it be that the Savior has an inheritance in the saints? Indeed, these are the very words of the Apostle.

We have often sung:

> When by His grace I shall look on His face,
> That will be glory for me.

Is it possible that we could change the song and scripturally sing?

> When through His grace He shall look in our face,
> That will be glory for Him.

Yes, God has chosen a people as an inheritance for His Son. Following are two passages of Scripture which for a better name we call the "Convergence of Hope."

"I shall be satisfied, when I awake, with Thy likeness" (Ps. 17:15). *This is the expectation of the saint.*

"He shall see of the travail of His soul, and shall be satisfied" (Is. 53:11). *This is the expectation of the Savior.*

What a wonderful day will that day be when both Savior and saints are satisfied! The inheritance of the Savior is the saints, they form it and are its peculiar glory. This purchase is for a purpose entirely redounding to His glory.

To be sure, William Lincoln is right when he says: "God has everything,—glory, grace,—but He wants vessels, and that is what He has in us."

God was not satisfied in possessing suns and stars, He wanted sons and saints. He has them in us. Christ desired more than to be the creator of suns and stars and systems. *He made a new creation of sons and saints* and these we are.

In these saints Christ has riches of glory, fullness of glory, effulgence of glory, outflowing, overflowing glory, prodigality of glory, which is yet to flood the universe. Certainly we cannot understand, therefore the apostle Paul prays that we may. Whatever glory this is, it is all to the praise of the glory of His grace.

O God, open our eyes to know "what is the riches of the glory of His inheritance in the saints"!

3. The Third "What"

"What is the exceeding greatness of His power?"

The Apostle also desires that our eyes may be opened to know "what is the exceeding greatness of His power to usward who believe."

Power is the one thing the *church* of God *needs most* and has least. The work of the Lord languishes for lack of power. The church, like Samson in the lap of a harlot, has divulged the secret of strength and is shorn of power. The church cannot arise and go out as at other times, and this the Philistines well know.

O that Paul's prayer were answered, that the church should have open eyes to realize and recognize the present working of His power.

Dr. A. T. Pierson has called attention to God's standard of power in the two Testaments. In the Old Testament the measurement by which God worked in behalf of His people was "like as it was to Israel in the day that he came up out of the land of Egypt" (Is. 11:16). When God desired to call attention to His power in their behalf, it was in calling to their remembrance what God did when He brought them out of Egypt. This seems to be the supreme display of His power during the Old Testament period.

There is a *new standard* of power in the New Testament. Not as "when I brought Israel out of Egypt," but *when Christ was raised* from the dead.

The Apostle declares that God's power to usward is

according to the working of His mighty power, which He wrought in Christ, when He raised Him from the dead, and set Him at His own right hand in the heavenly places, far above all principality, and power, and might, and dominion and every name that is named, not only in this world, but also in that which is to come (Eph. 1:19-21).

This is God's New Testament standard. The Apostle desires that our eyes may be opened to understand it.

When God raised Christ from the dead and exalted Him to His own right hand, He established a new standard of power. It was power transcending anything previously revealed. It was great power that brought Israel out of Egypt and dealt with the material elements which intervened as obstacles, but much in excess of this was God's display of power when He raised Christ up from the dead.

Wherein was the resurrection of Christ from the dead "exceeding greatness and power"? That Christ should be raised from the dead was no secret. The Old Testament bore this prophecy and held forth this promise. The Apostle says, "Christ rose again on the third day according to the Scriptures" (1 Cor. 15:4). But wherein was the exceeding greatness of this power? After what manner was a hyperbole established?

The secret of power which the Apostle desires the Ephesians to know and the supreme knowledge that should be possessed by the Church of God lies at exactly this point. The power which God displayed at the resurrection of Christ, when He raised Him up from the dead and seated Him at His own right hand, is in this, that He not only raised up Christ from the dead and seated Him, but that He also simultaneously *raised us up together with Him and seated us together with Him* (Eph. 2:5, 6). O to God, let praises swell!

Christ had died for our sins. With Him we went to His death. He could not leave us there, for with Him we arose in His life, but He could not leave us there, for with Him we were raised into heavenly places, "far above all principality and power, and might, and dominion," and He will not leave us there, for "when Christ who is our Life shall appear, then shall we also appear with Him in glory!" Let praises unto God arise.

Nor is this all that is implied in the "exceeding greatness" of power in Christ when He raised Him from the dead, for we cannot overlook the little word "us," for the us here refers to both Jew and Gentile. He not only got us together, but He raised us up together and the *only place in the universe which we know of Jew and Gentile being one* is the place in Christ to which we have been raised up together.

11

JEW AND GENTILE "TOGETHER"
Ephesians 2:1-22

WE HAVE BEEN lost in wonder and amazement at the display of Divine power exercised in the resurrection of Christ from the dead and His exaltation *to* the right hand of God.

We found its power and potentiality consisted not only in the resurrection of Christ from the death to which our sin had borne Him, but in that He who went to the cross *for us* arose from the dead *with us*. We were quickened "together with Christ," "raised up together" and "made to sit together" (Eph. 2:5, 6).

"Quickened us together," "raised us up together," and "made us to sit together." Note the "us." The "us" here is the *Jew and the Gentile* who are now "*one in Christ Jesus*" and are "one" in the Church which is His Body, in which Body none are reckoned as Jews and none are reckoned as Gentiles. Both are "one in Christ Jesus." This is the first time the Jew and the Gentile were ever together. The only place in the universe you can get the Jew and the Gentile together is "in Christ Jesus." In fact, the Jew and the Gentile were Divinely separated. God made choice of Israel (Deut. 32:9) and separated this nation from the nations. This national separation was to be maintained throughout their national history.

Lo, the people shall dwell alone and shall not be reckoned among the nations (Num. 23:9).

Their aloofness and aloneness was of Divine ordering. They were separated from the Gentiles by a "middle wall of partition" (Eph. 2:14). It was a barrier Divinely erected. This wall was to shut *Israel in* and the *Gentiles out*. The separation and preservation of Israel was necessary to God's purpose. It was not a display of favoritism on the part of God, for God is "no respecter of persons." Rather it was that *ultimately blessing might come to all the nations.* God made choice for a channel. The individuality of the Jew and the Gentile, nationally speaking, is to be maintained to the end of human history. At present and in the Church, the Body of Christ, God is not dealing with either Jew or Gentile nationally. Israel has been temporarily set aside and the Gentiles are placed on the waiting list, as their blessing must come through Israel.

The Epistle to the Ephesians is concerned particularly with the Church which is God's provision for the crisis. The believing Jew and Gentile are *one Body in Christ*. The Ephesian letter gives emphasis to this fact and explains the Divine method by which it is accomplished.

The cross is the measurement of all of God's mercies! It contains all sufficiency for every and any crisis. The cross is the power of God and the wisdom of God. It is the medium of manifestation of any and all the attributes of God. The cross reaches to all lengths, possesses all strength and has within it all the requirements of Divine strategy! No blessing can ever come to any person, persons or peoples, at any time or anywhere in all the universe of God, apart from the cross of Christ.

The cross is the instrument of any judgment whatsoever which may ever come to any person, persons or peoples at any place, any time in the universe! God dealt with sin at the cross and it is the cross which fixes the ultimate destiny of both the believer and the unbeliever. What Christ accomplished at the cross is *as final* as it is *finished*. Whatever reconciliation is effected between Jew and Gentile is the work of the cross. It is the foundation of all dispensation and the ground of all grace in Divine government.

The "middle wall of partition" (Eph. 2:14) was removed by means of the cross. Christ's death was sufficient for the dilemma, closed up the division and revealed the character of the dispensation now present. Here is the record of this wonderful reconciliation.

> For He is our peace, who hath made both one, and hath broken down the middle wall of partition between us; having abolished in His flesh the enmity, even the law of commandments, contained in ordinances; for to make in Himself of twain one new man, so making peace; and that He might reconcile both unto God in one Body by the cross, having slain the enmity thereby; and came and preached peace to you which were afar off, and to them that were nigh. For through Him we both have access by one Spirit unto the Father (Eph. 2:14-18).

Thus we behold the Jew and the Gentile "in one Body by the cross" (2:16). God has by fusion brought to a glorious end seeming confusion and this is called "*His workmanship.*" It is a "creation in Christ Jesus." It is indeed God's "masterpiece." *Jew and Gentile now sing together as one,* "He is our peace, who hath made both one, and hath broken down the middle wall of partition between us" (2:14).

That which made them twain is now slain and the result is "one new man." The Gentile was not raised up to the position of the Jew nor the Jew brought down to the position of the Gentile, but they both, without reference to the liabilities of the one or the disabilities of the other, are "raised up together" to a place and position transcending any promise previously published to either!

In Christ, the Jew is not at an advantage nor is the Gentile at a disadvantage.

There is a wonderful contrast in the Disabilities of the Gentiles and the Liabilities of Israel.

See them here in distinguishing display:

THE DISABILITIES OF THE GENTILES (Ephesians 2:11, 12)	THE LIABILITIES OF THE JEW (Romans 9:4)
1. "Gentiles" (v. 11)	1. "Who are Israelites" (v. 4)
2. "Uncircumcision" (v. 11)	2. "The Adoption" (v. 4)
3. "Without Christ" (v. 12)	3. "The Glory" (v. 4)
4. "Aliens from the Commonwealth of Israel" (v. 12)	4. "The Covenants" (v. 4)
5. "Strangers from the Covenants" (v. 12)	5. "The Law" (v. 4)
6. "Having no Hope" (v. 12)	6. "The Services" (v. 4)
7. "Without God" (v. 12)	7. "The Promises" (Prophecies) (v. 4)

A glance at the balance sheet above will show much to Israel's credit. While the assets of Israel are great, so also are the liabilities. The disabilities of the Gentiles are appalling. Certainly the above presents a vast difference and degree of distinction.

In the Epistle to the Romans in chapter 1 we have the *Gentiles* to whom God had made Primeval Revelation through His Work (Rom. 1:19, 20). This revelation was not received and the judgment of condemnation is passed upon them and they are declared by God to be "*without excuse*" (Rom. 1:20).

In the second chapter of Romans the *Jew* to whom God made Permanent Revelation in His Word, is also judged guilty with the verdict, "*inexcusable*" (Rom. 2:1).

In the third chapter of Romans the *Jew and Gentile are both judged guilty* with the Divine declaration, "there is no difference, for all have sinned" (Rom. 3:22, 23).

Both Jew and Gentile were sinners because they had both come from the same and single person, Adam, and from one source. So also in Ephesians, God does not deal with distinctions and differences as privilege did not prevent guilt, neither does it merit grace. Grace reckons neither with merit or demerit for then it would cease to be grace. It would be of debt and degree and these are never known to grace. It is not a question of the law, for grace is manifested apart from law.

It is not a question of lawlessness, for grace abounds beyond all such. It is not a question of good works, for grace is manifested apart from works. The *glory of grace* is, that man's sin cannot hinder it or his good works help it. It is grace and grace is always grace or it ceases to be grace.

Thus, regardless of their past or their privileges, the Jew and the Gentile are one by the work of the cross. While one formerly had access to God through the veil, the other was kept afar off in the court of the Gentiles, now, through Him they both have "access by one Spirit unto the Father" (Eph. 2:18). Upon the basis of Christ's death, peace is preached to "you which were afar off" (Gentiles) and "to them that were nigh" (Jews) (Eph. 2:17).

They are not foreigners now; they are fellow-citizens. The "exceeding greatness" of the power which God wrought in Christ when He raised Him from the dead is, in that He raised the Jew and Gentile "up together" and seated them "together in heavenly places in Christ" (2:6). But not in that elevation and exaltation to be known in the future as in the past, by racial distinctions, but as "one in Christ Jesus," nor does this by any means infer that hereafter God will not deal with Israel as a nation or with the Gentiles as nations. Such is not the case for God will resume the former national relations at the close of the present dispensation.

Unfortunate indeed is the chapter division coming between verse 23 of chapter 1, and the first verse of chapter 2. Verse 1, second chapter, is a continuation of the Apostle's argument and undoubtedly follows 1:20 in marvelous unity and continuity.

At the close of chapter 1, Christ is raised from the dead and seated at God's own right hand, but not only Christ, but Christ "*and you.*" And "you hath He quickened who were dead in trespasses and sins" (Eph. 2:1). With what triumphant and telling force the Holy Spirit employs the words, "and you." The exaltation of Christ is not apart from "you." See another blessed example of this "and you," in Colossians:

And, having made peace through the blood of His cross, by Him to reconcile all things unto Himself; by Him, I say, whether they be things in earth, or things in heaven, *and you,* that were sometime alienated and enemies in your mind by wicked works, yet now hath He reconciled in the body of His flesh through death, to present you holy and unblamable and unreprovable in His sight (Col. 1:20-22).

In both Ephesians and Colossians the Holy Spirit singularly stresses the bestowment of God's grace upon the Gentiles. They are first mentioned here, as when Christ had risen and sent word for a meeting of His disciples "and Peter."

This Epistle which is addressed to Gentiles speaks in this chapter first of them (vv. 1, 2), then of the Jew (v. 3), then of what God had done for both—they were both "quickened together," "raised up together," and "seated together" with Christ (2:5, 6). The last portion of this chapter reveals the manner and method by which this wonderful reconciliation took place.

In verses 1 and 2, the Jew and the Gentile are shown alike to be sinners. We believe the "you" and the "ye" in verses 1 and 2 refer primarily to the Gentiles and the "we" and "our" in verse 3, to the Jew. The self-righteous Jew was the same in God's sight as the despised Gentile. In judgment God concluded them both under sin with "no difference." In love He raised them both up together with no division. They are "one in Christ Jesus." They by nature, both stood guilty before God. The privileges of the one or the poverty of the other did not affect grace in the least. In grace they share the same standing before God for by grace came their salvation. The merit of one or the demerit of the other counts for nothing.

At this point we would give place to a twofold exhortation:

First, let the student remember that the union, of Jew and Gentile into one Body, is under discussion in this chapter. The Jew and Gentile by the death, burial and resurrection of Christ were raised from their natural sinful condition, to be one in Christ. A contrast between their past positions reveals *inequality.* Their sinful natures reveal *equality.* The death of

Christ was for both alike and both became, in this dispensation of God's great grace, *equal sharers in Christ!*

Second: Let us remember the Bible is not a book of synonyms. If it were, where then would or could interpretation be established? Words are not used interchangeably in the Scriptures; if so, then why "words which the Holy Spirit speaketh"? In this Divine Book of sixty-six portions, God says what He means and means what He says. For this reason let us study carefully the "ye" and the "we" of this passage now in consideration. Remember that God is dealing with both Jew and Gentile of whom He hath made one Body.

Question: Is *Body* the only relation of the Church mentioned in Ephesians? We think not. A close study will reveal *four figures* in Ephesians, viz., *Body, Building, Bride* and *Bivouac.* These we will consider in due time.

The Condition of the Gentiles

At the close of chapter 1, we saw a "working." It was the working of God in the resurrection of Christ. This is called the "working of His mighty power" (1:19).

In chapter 2, there is another "working." The person working is the "prince of the power of the air" (2:2). He worked in the Ephesians as he now works in all the unbelieving and disobedient. The spirit of the "prince of the power of the air," says the Apostle, "now worketh" (v. 2). The character, course and conduct of the present age is under his control. This place he will hold until the consummation of this dispensation. From this person and his power those addressed in this Epistle had been delivered. They had been delivered from "this present evil world,"—it was the will of God (Gal. 1:4). They who boast of being abreast of the "spirit of the times," little realize that the spirit of this time is the spirit of the "prince of the power of the air." Indeed those who thus boast are of this self-same person and under his power.

The believer has but one boast, but one object of glory, that is "the cross." The glory with which they glory in the cross is that by the cross they are dead to the age and the age is dead unto them (Gal. 6:14). The Christian has nothing to do with the present sinful order of things. The present order is at discord with the will of God. Three things are said of their past thraldom.

1. "Dead in trespasses and sins" (Eph. 2:1)
2. "Walked according to the course of this age" (v. 2)
3. "Walked according to the prince of the power of the air" (v. 2)

Certainly the deepest depths are in Ephesians, as are also the highest heights. They were dead to God and alive unto sin. They walked "according to the course of this age." The Greek word used here for "world" is *aion*. In most of the former passages the word *cosmos* is translated "world." They walked "according to the course of this age." What is the course of this age? What of its tend, trend and end? Is it spiritual or satanic? Is it of God or of men? Is it in a state of uplift or downfall? Is it in a process of evolution or does it bear the seeds of revolution? Is it moving upward to Christ or onward to antichrist? Does the present trend prophesy triumph or tribulation? Is this age an age of faith or an age of flesh? Does it love science or Scripture? Is its boast in "thus saith the Lord" or, thus doeth man? Does it respect law or does it receive lawlessness? Who is the God of this age and can the age be in character a thing apart from him, and can its end be otherwise than his end? What a terrible thing it is to walk according to the course of the age!

But were the Jews better for their privileges? Not one whit, for they came from the same source, *fallen Adam.*

"And were *by nature* the children of wrath, even as others" (Eph. 2:3).

The peculiar force of "even as others" should not be overlooked. The Jew had sufficient advantage that if there was anything good in man he would not be "even as others." The Jew was "even as others" because he was "even as others." What we mean is well expressed by Bishop Moule, who when commenting on the words "also we all" (v. 3) says:

"Saint Paul often insists on this *one* level of fallen nature."*

Let us recall that in Romans 1, the Gentile is guilty before God and "without excuse." In Romans 2 the Jew is guilty before God and "inexcusable." In Romans 3 both Jew and Gentile are concluded "guilty" and every mouth shut. In Romans, chapter 5, we find the cause. It is because "in Adam all sinned,"—both Jew and Gentile. One was no better than the other and the other no worse, for all had sin in one and were one in sin. For this cause they are now in Christ Jesus. Paul says in Ephesians 2:3, *But God who is rich in mercy,* has "quickened us together" and "raised us up together" and made us "sit together." Condemned in sin "together" and raised with Christ "together."

O the glory of the Gospel of grace which lays the foundation of the Gospel of glory!

O God, we who write and we who read, thank Thee, that "times past" are times past and forever past!

O the Divine tenses of Ephesians 2!

Times past! Dead in trespasses and sin, walking according to the course of this age, under the authority of the prince of the air, living in the lust of the flesh and by nature children appointed to the coming day of wrath—"but now" the *present tense,* "raised and seated with Christ," and then, the *future tense,* "in the ages to come" set forth to display the riches of His grace! Let us who are so lifted, be bowed low! How rich grace is, will be best seen in the union of the Jew and Gentile in one Body in Christ!

Glory be to the Father and to the Son and to the Holy Ghost! Amen.

Before we proceed in our study of the Epistle to the Ephesians to that portion which is introduced at the opening of the third chapter, a *review and retrospect* here will result in our blessing.

---

*H. C. G. Moule, *Studies in Ephesians* (Grand Rapids: Kregel Publications, 1977), p. 69.

In parsing the wonderful sentence which began with verse 3 of chapter 1, and concluded with verse 14 of the same chapter, we discovered that "in the dispensation of the fulness of times" God had purposed to "gather together in one, all things in Christ" (1:10).

The word "together" was there introduced and if the student will recall, this word, "together," has been much before us in these studies. Ephesians is the Epistle in which things get "together." In the "gathering" of things "together" the first step is, as we have seen to be largely the contents of chapters 1 and 2, the bringing "together" of the Jew and the Gentile. A summary will reveal the following:

1. The Jew and Gentile were dead in sin "together."
2. The Jew and the Gentile were raised up "together."
3. The Jew and the Gentile were made to "sit together."
4. Their union resulted in a building fitly "framed together."
5. They were "builded together" for an habitation of God.

Thus we see a marvelous getting "together" which resulted in unity and oneness. Separated portions coming together into unity make for oneness and this "oneness" was also proclaimed in verse 10 (chap. 1)—"that He might gather together in 'one' all things in Christ." We have not only found often occurring the use of the word "together," but also the word "one."

1. "He is our peace who hath made both *one*" (2:14).
2. "Having abolished in His flesh the enmity, ... for to make in Himself of twain *one* new man" (2:15).
3. "And that He might reconcile both unto God in *one* Body by the cross" (2:16).
4. "For through Him we both have access by *one* spirit unto the Father" (2:18).

The scattered things are being gathered together into *one* and this work will continue until the dissolution and separation brought about by sin and death is no more. What God commenced here will be continued until the consummation!

We now approach the study of the "Mystery," the way for which having been made ready in the preceding studies.

This is amply indicated by the opening words of the Apostle in Ephesians 3:1. There is unity and continuity throughout the Epistle. Says the Apostle Paul, "According as I have written before briefly" (3:3). Evidently referring to the things in the preceding paragraph, from 2:13 to the end of the second chapter.

The ministry of the "mystery" is now before us. It begins with the *prisoner* and ends with the *prayer*. It begins with the *disclosure,* and ends with the *doxology.* How precious this portion! God open our eyes in answer to the former prayer of the apostles in Ephesians 1:18 and following.

12

THE MESSENGER AND THE MYSTERY
Ephesians 3:1-9

WE SEE AT the opening of the chapter The Messenger (3:1-7); then The Mystery (vv. 8, 9), and last, The Measurements (v. 18) (see page 110).

For this ministry of the Mystery, special Divine choice was made of an instrument through whom it should be made known,—this instrument was the apostle Paul. Having not been originally chosen among the twelve, he is permitted to make known things the twelve never knew. They walked with Christ in His earthly ministry, Paul's apostleship is related to the Living Christ in the glory, and it is in no way strange that things in the heavenlies should be the subject of His ministry and testimony.

The Messenger

He whose call is from heaven is permitted to speak of a *calling* which is in heaven. Unto him was committed a "dispensation," a stewardship. God made him responsible for a "revelation" of which we are recipients. This mystery was given unto him by "*revelation*" (v. 3). It was not the subject of any prophecy or any previous writings. Search where you will in Divine writings, you will not find this which is especially committed to him. There is nothing of it in the Old Testament from Moses to Malachi, or from the Pentateuch to the Prophets. Nor is it to be found in the writings of the other apostles. It is Divinely and distinctively Paul's for publication. It was special truth committed to him as a sacred trust. He referred to it at another time as a "deposit." He was its administrator. It was not given for his own information and inspiration, but for immediate publication, "which is given me toward you" (v. 2).

'In other ages it was not made known unto the sons of men, as it is now revealed unto His holy apostles and prophets by the Spirit" (v. 5). It will be well to compare the "but now" of Ephesians 2:13 with the "is now" of Ephesians 3:5. Of course the "holy apostles and prophets" are New Testament apostles and prophets, and the apostles here mentioned are to be understood as New Testament prophets. There is no contradiction here nor confusion, nor is there any confounding of Old Testament office with New Testament order. F. W. Grant at this point speaks helpfully:

> He writes, after his manner, the names of others along with himself, and these, no doubt, were the dispensers under him of that which was to him, first of all, a personal revelation.

Notice also the beauty of the words, "as it is now revealed unto His holy apostles and prophets by the Spirit." It is the Holy Spirit who makes it known unto us. Paul may be the instrument to proclaim it, but the Spirit of God must make it known. One may hear and not know,—the knowledge of the "mystery" must be brought to us by that blessed Spirit of God. He is not only the *Sealer* as we saw Him in 1:13, but He is also the *Revealer of Secrets* as here declared.

The Mystery

What is the "mystery"? It behooves us to be careful here, for it is possible to make the "mystery" a mystery. It is possible to cause to be concealed what God has revealed. Let us remember the "mystery" is a "revelation," not a riddle. It is something made known, not something covered up. It was "hidden in God," but is now manifest. In this "mystery" there is nothing which savors of the black art or the mystically mysterious. There are none of the vagaries of Gnosticism with which the Epistle to the Colossians so vigorously deals. It is not referring to things secretly hidden within veils and surrounded with interrogation and suspicion. The mystery of Ephesians is revealed plainly and particularly. The Greek word does not indicate the mysterious. It is knowledge for the initiated. It means something *not known until shown,* rather than something which is unknown.

Those "in Christ" may understand, not only so, but a standing "in Christ" is the only possible place of understanding. That which was "hidden in God" was hidden from man until God wills to make it known. He now wills to make it known, and this is all the mystery with which we should surround the "mystery." We do not need the key to a house which is open.

What the mystery is, is plainly stated in Ephesians 3:6:

"That the Gentiles
  1. Should be fellow heirs,
  2. and of the same Body
  3. and partakers of his promise in Christ by the Gospel."

We have thus separated the three clauses of this verse for classification. The use of the word "and" here admits of and justifies, we believe, such a division. Three things are before us for consideration and, we trust, serious and spiritual meditation; and remember, in the unfolding of this passage, we are to see as its ultimate purpose the enlarging of the circle, which is to bring about the "gathering together in one, all things in Him." For the force of this mystery is a "fellowship." Of these things we do not dare speak until verses 9 and 10 have been reached.

At verse 6 of chapter 3 we find the "mystery" plainly stated. Three things are embraced, viz.: "That the Gentiles (1) should be fellow heirs, (2) and of the same Body, (3) and partakers of his promise in Christ by the Gospel." Let these three things be further considered.

Here begins the unfolding of the unimagined contents of this wonderful revelation vouchsafed unto Paul. It concerns "Gentiles" and such were the Ephesians, and he was an "apostle to the Gentiles" and had been given grace to "preach among the Gentiles the unsearchable riches of Christ" (see 3:8). With what spiritual refreshing this special message came to them. In times past they were dependent upon Israel for their blessing. This was the Divine plan published from the beginning. God said unto Abraham, "In thee shall all *families* of the earth be blessed" (Gen. 12:3). The very geographical position of the nations on the map of the habitable world was in relation to Israel (Deut. 32:8).

The one nation, Israel, was the Divinely chosen channel for national blessing. How well the Gentiles understood this is illustrated often throughout the Scriptures, but nowhere more vividly than in Matthew 15:21-28. It is the Evangelist's record of the visit of the Syro-Phœnician woman to Jesus. We see *first:* The Woman, Her Daughter, and Her Desire; *second:* The Savior, His Silence and Severity; *third:* The Woman, Her Daughter and Deliverance. How seemingly severe was the Savior when this Gentile woman called upon Him as the "Son of David," upon whom as a Gentile, she had no claim. He had come to the "lost sheep of the house of Israel" and she was not of this "house." She was not a child of the "promise." The ministry of Messiah was not for her first, but for the "Jew first," and then the Gentile. He came to "His own" (John 1:11). He came to save "His people" (Matt. 1:21) and the only people called "His people" were those of Israel. How often throughout the Old Testament Jehovah cries, "My people." See notable example in the cry of Jehovah in Isaiah 1:3, "My people doth not consider." See also, "My vineyard" in Isaiah 5. The purpose of Messiah's ministry and manifestation is clearly stated in Romans 15:8.

> Now I say that Jesus Christ was a minister of the *circumcision* for the truth of God, to confirm the *promises* made unto the fathers.

The Syro-Phœnician woman was not of the "circumcision" and was a "stranger" to the "covenants of promise" made to the "fathers" and was without immediate claim upon the "Son of David." But she knew if He blessed "the children," then blessing would follow on and flow out to her as a Gentile, for this was the Divine order.

Jesus clearly and forcefully stated the object of His ministry when He said, "It is not meet to take the children's bread and cast it to dogs" (Matt. 15:26). How remarkable was her wisdom and how keen her wit, for she said, "Truth, Lord: yet the dogs eat of the crumbs which fall from their master's table" (Matt. 15:27). O that glorious title, "Lord," it leaps over the wall with which the title, "Son of David," surrounded Israel. She well understood the primacy and privilege of Israel, but she also knew that Gentile blessing followed subsequently upon Israel's fullness. (This is all changed now for Israel's blessing now awaits the fullness of the Gentiles. See Rom. 11:25.)

The blessing of the Gentiles through the blessing of Israel is always true when God is dealing nationally. It has been true in the past and will be true in the future, but is not true in Ephesians, for here God is not dealing nationally with either Israel or the Gentiles. They are "fellow heirs" in the Church— neither having precedence nor privilege, but are of the "same Body" and are "partakers" together of an eternal purpose of God in Christ. This is the message of the mystery. This was not made known in other ages. It was "hidden in God." That which was concealed is now revealed. It would have astounded any Old Testament prophet to have been told that there would ever be a dispensation in which the Jew and Gentile would be "fellow heirs" and of the "same Body." It was nowhere traceable in the Old Testament. This is, we believe, the "unsearchable riches" of Ephesians. That God would bless Israel and through them the Gentiles was plainly discernible throughout the Old Testament, but *this marvelous union and unity* was given unto Paul *for revelation* when the time was due. And how harmonious is all this with Ephesians as a whole. In chapters 1—3 we have the *Heavenly Calling,* in chapters 4 and 5 the *Heavenly Conduct,* and in chapter 6, the *Heavenly Conflict.* We began in our study of Ephesians with "all spiritual blessings in heavenly places." The revelation of the mystery through the ministry of Paul is in full harmony with the "heavenly calling" of Ephesians.

For the sake of illustration let us imagine the following: It is announced that a Navajo Indian, who is swift on foot, is to be entered in a speed contest against an airplane to a given goal. Of course, the Indian must run his race upon the earth, for in the very nature of his being, he cannot run anywhere else. The airplane must take its course through the trackless air, for in the nature of its organization, it cannot do otherwise. The Indian was adapted to the earth and the airplane to the air. Which of the two may be more easily traced and tracked, the Indian or the airplane? The Indian would leave his trail upon the earth and could be easily tracked through his journey from the beginning to the end, for his race is on the earth. The airplane, which traveled in the heavens, *left no trace whatever.*

The history of Israel, past, present and future, is easily traced, but the Church, which is of heavenly calling and heavenly vocation, cannot be traced. In fact, that there was to be such a body was wholly unthought of. There was nothing in the history of Israel or of the nations to indicate such a joint fellowship and heirship as revealed in this Epistle. Unquestionably it was mentioned by Christ, but was manifested through Paul.

Note the triple fellowship brought out by the Revised Version in which the rendering of this sixth verse is as follows: "That the Gentiles are "fellow heirs, fellow members of the Body and fellow partakers of the promise in Christ through the Gospel." Notice—fellow heirs, fellow members, fellow partakers. Paul was the Divine instrument, but what was the Divine intention, for the "mystery" was embraced in the Divine purpose and proposition which we found early in the study of Ephesians, namely: "In the dispensation of the fulness of times, He might gather together in one all things in Christ, both which are in heaven and which are on earth."

The student will easily see that it is impossible throughout

Ephesians to get away from the first utterances of the wonderful sentence which we found beginning at 1:3 and ending at 1:14. We shall, by the help of God, and the illumination of the Spirit of inspiration, seek to ascertain the Divine purpose in the revelation of the mystery.

To what purpose has God made Jews and Gentiles, "fellow heirs and of the same Body"? If we have learned that He blessed Israel that He might bless the Gentile nations of the earth, is it not possible that if we see blended and blessed together in one Body, both Jew and Gentile, it is for blessing of yet other of God's creatures? If, through Israel, the earth was to be blessed, is it possible that through the Church, blessing is to come to creatures in the heavenlies? How deep is all this, yet how Divine! Can it be possible this is the "riches of the revelation"?

13

THE DISPLAY OF GOD'S GRACE
Ephesians 3:10, 11

To the intent that now unto the principalities and powers in heavenly places might be known by the Church the manifold wisdom of God, according to the eternal purpose which He purposed in Christ Jesus our Lord (Ephesians 3:10, 11).

ALL OF GOD'S benevolence is for creature blessing. He never makes revelation without reason. His program works always to His purpose. Nowhere is this Divine discretion on greater display than in His Divine choice of the Church and the calling of the same. We have seen that God's provision for the earth and its blessing is ample in Israel. The "families of the earth" may rest assured that, in God's choice of Israel, their ultimate blessing is certain.

But the peoples that dwell on the earth are not the only creatures of God which come within His love and purpose. Nor is the earth the only sphere which is to receive the benefits of Christ's redeeming and reconciling work. The spheres to which the redemptive and reconciliatory work of Christ extends are three: "Heaven," "Earth," and "Under the Earth." See Colossians 1:20 and also Philippians 2:10, "In heaven—in earth—under the earth." The last book of the Canon of Holy Scriptures, the Book of Revelation, is found to be a series of events taking place in "Heaven," in "Earth," and in chapter 9—"under the earth."

The scope and sphere of both God's salvations and God's condemnations are but little understood.

When God made choice of the Church, it was for an "intent." "To the intent," says the Apostle. What is the intent?—"that now unto the principalities and powers in heavenly places might be made known by the Church, the manifold wisdom of God" (Eph. 3:10).

The word "now" is often used in this letter to the Ephesians. Concerning this, G. Campbell Morgan said:

> The word "now," recurring more than once in the course of this letter, does not indicate immediateness of time, but introduces the statement of a result of a previous process.

This is undoubtedly true, for the force of the word "now" is in that through the Divine call and choice of the Church, provision which was previously unknown is now made manifest. The word "now" by no means limits the display of God's wisdom to "principalities and powers" through the Church, to the dispensation now present. Its reference is also to the future.

A summary of the situation as revealed in Ephesians is as follows:

The *Secret* of the Church was "hidden in God" (Eph. 3:2, 5, 9).

The *Scale* of the calling of the Church was "according to an eternal purpose" (Eph. 3:11).

The *Sphere* of the calling of the Church is into "heavenly places" (Eph. 1:3).

The *Service* of the Church is unto "principalities and powers in heavenly places" (Eph. 3:10).

The *Strife* of the Church is "against principalities and powers in heavenly places" (Eph. 6:12).

The *Scope* of the ministry of the Church is to the "ages to come" (Eph. 2:7).

Thus we see that throughout the Epistle to the Ephesians the sphere is always "heavenly places." In previous chapters we discovered that "heavenly places" or the "heavenlies" is a fixed locality. We also learned that the premundane calling of the Church marked out for it a supermundane ministry. The ministry of Israel is unto the earth. The ministry of the Church is in the heavenlies. Thus we see the ever-widening circles of the benevolence and blessing of God to His creatures. We are of the earth,—earthly, and how little we know of things in the heavenlies. In our selfishness we would contain and consume the love of God and the benefits of the cross upon ourselves, little realizing that if God lavished upon us love, it was that through us, He might publish His own glorious acts and attributes unto others.

Apart from His person, God's greatest glory is the glory He bestows upon His creatures. But is Adam's fallen race the sum total of the creatures to whom He would minister? By no means! And is it from the redeemed of Adam's race alone He is to receive honor and glory? By no means! It is the Divine intention, "unto principalities and powers in heavenly places," to display His "manifold wisdom" and His own glorious character.

Can it be possible that Gentiles, who had come to such ruin as Romans, chapter 1, and Ephesians, chapter 2 reveals; and Jews of such character as Romans, chapter 2 indicates to us,—is it possible, we say, that these, between whom there was no difference in nature, should be, by grace "raised up together," "seated together," "built together as members of the same Body," in coming ages be exhibited in "heavenly places unto principalities and powers," as a display of the variegated and manifold wisdom of God? *Yes, it is true,* for the *will* of God has purposed it; the *work* of Christ has performed it, and the *Word* of God has proclaimed it.

If we "speak of earthly things," very few understand. There is dense ignorance on every hand concerning God's earthly purpose in Israel; but when we come to speak of "heavenly things" as related to the Church and her distinct calling, we seem "to speak as fools." Indeed we speak not as fools but as wise,—"wisdom which the Holy Spirit teacheth." With what distortion and contortion the Holy Scriptures are handled!

What confusion is therefore brought upon us! The Church of God in ignorance, seeks to fulfil the vocation of Israel upon the earth, thus usurping Israel's calling which issues not only in criminal neglect to Israel but also in spiritual disaster to the Church.

In our study of the Epistle to the Ephesians with what force is the Apostle's prayer brought to us again and again,—"that the eyes of your understanding being enlightened; that ye may know what is the hope of His calling, and what the riches of the glory of His inheritance in the saints" (Ephesians 1:18). The saints do not know the hope of their calling,—they do not know what is "His inheritance in them." This the Epistle to the Ephesians reveals and there is necessity of a widespread revival in the study of the Church Epistles. Wouldn't it be wise for every believer to enroll in class study for one year in the Epistles of Paul? Why not a few months' study of the "risen Christ, His risen people, and His heavenly purpose"?

Remember that *through the Church* "unto principalities and powers" *God will make a display* of His "manifold wisdom,"—wisdom in many phases and at many angles.

He will display His wisdom in setting aside national Israel for a season and the calling of the Jew and the Gentile into one Body during that period of Israel's national rejection.

He will display the Divine wisdom of choosing the Church from *before* the foundation of the world that there should be no conflict with Israel whom He chose *from* the foundation of the world.

He will display His Divine wisdom and grace which takes no cognizance of the merits of the Jew or the demerits of the Gentile, but reckons them as one for an eternal purpose.

He will reveal His own glorious character in that He is just and the justifier of them that believe in Jesus.

He will display how the jarring attributes of God met together at the cross,—"Mercy and truth are met together; righteousness and peace have kissed each other" (Ps. 85:10).

He will display the manner in which His sacrifice on the

cross completely sustained His holiness of character and the love and mercy of His heart.

He will display how mercy rejoiced over judgment. Indeed through the Church every phase of His wisdom in creation and redemption will be on display. It will be the marvel of created intelligences in heavenly places of which we now know but little and are left standing all amazed. It is an unthought of honor! It is an unthought of glory!

It is but little wonder that wicked hosts in "heavenly places" are at present waging warfare against the Church, knowing as they do that in the heavenly places in which they now hold dominion, the Church will soon be on display.

The very conflict of the Church indicates the calling of the Church. The present strife of the Church marks out the future sphere of the Church. The wealth of the Church may be, in some degree, estimated by the warfare now waged against the Church. Wicked hosts in heavenly places have made the Church the objective of their hate for a twofold reason: *Usurpation* and *Revelation.* At the coming of the Lord wicked spiritual hosts will be driven from their location in "the heavenlies" and their place will be occupied by the Church. By this they shall suffer not only *usurpation* of *position,* but of *power* also.

In the realm or sphere where these wicked hosts have held governmental sway, we believe the Church will display in grace, the "manifold wisdom of God." The mystery of iniquity reaches to the heights as well as to the depths. The dominion of the devil is not confined to the earth alone, but to "things in heaven" and "under the earth" also. "We (of the Church) wrestle not against flesh and blood" (Eph. 6:12). Ours is a more subtle warfare, if such could be. Ours is a conflict against the wicked hosts of the "heavenly places" to which God has called us.

Since the time when God, through the apostle Paul, made known the secret of the calling of the Church, these enemies have sought to overthrow the Church and refute the Divine purpose. First, by blinding the eyes of the Church to the hope of her glorious calling and by seducing her conduct to that which is unbecoming a heavenly calling. As to what success Satan has achieved, one may easily behold the present fallen state of the Church. Paul prays that the Church may have open eyes to know the "calling" and its "hope" (Eph. 1:18) and exhorts the Church to walk in the hope of the calling (Eph. 4:1, 2). This is the remedy required and the remedy revealed. Today in many a pulpit and on many a platform this hope is ridiculed. The Church is charged with being too "other-worldly" and for this reason it is "this-worldly." The separation of the Church is its sanctification, all else is its humiliation and condemnation. May the Spirit of God show the Church that its end is translation, not reformation, and that the position of the Church is separation and not confederation.

14

PAUL'S SECOND PRAYER
Ephesians 3:14-21

ONCE AGAIN WE are to hear the apostle Paul pray! Let silence and sobriety take hold upon us for "behold he prayeth."

> For this cause I bow my knees unto the Father of our Lord Jesus Christ, of whom the whole family in heaven and earth is named. That He would grant you, according to the riches of His glory, to be strengthened with might by His Spirit in the inner man; that Christ may dwell in your hearts by faith; that ye, being rooted and grounded in love, may be able to comprehend with all saints what is the breadth, and length, and depth, and height; and to know the love of Christ, which passeth knowledge, that ye might be filled with all the fulness of God. Now unto Him that is able to do exceeding abundantly above all that we ask or think, according to the power that worketh in us. Unto Him be glory in the Church by Christ Jesus throughout all ages, world without end. Amen (Ephesians 3:14-21).

The First Prayer (1:17-23) followed the "eternal purpose" of God. So also does this Second Prayer (see 1:3-9, 11; 3:11).

In the study of Ephesians, whether in prayer or in practice, we are never outside the "eternal purpose." The "eternal purpose" is disclosed in these two prayers in a twofold aspect:

1. His eternal purpose in Himself concerning Christ;
2. His eternal purpose in Christ concerning the Church.

Christ and the Church are inseparable. Whatever is eternally purposed concerning one is vital to the destiny of the other.

These two prayers have also a bearing on the structure of the Ephesian Epistle. By them the Epistle is separated into its two parts and by them the doctrinal portion is developed and concluded. The opening statement of the argument of the Epistle is as follows: "Blessed be the *God and Father* of our Lord Jesus Christ." This is the beginning of that remarkable sentence which we sought to parse early in our study of this Epistle—a sentence extending from 1:3 to 1:14. From this sentence we are never able to escape. It lives in the very warp and woof of the entire Epistle. Its statements recur again and again. These two prayers follow the rule, and the first prayer is addressed to "God" and the second prayer to the "Father." There is remarkable unity and continuity in these two prayers. When compared this is eminently evident.

It is not so much the structure of this prayer that we desire to emphasize, but the substance. How apt one is, in the study of the Scriptures, to be concerned with the *letter* only, neglecting the *Spirit*. We must, however, be fully aware of the fact that apart from letter—the revealed Word—there is no spirit. The Holy Spirit rides triumphantly in the chariot of the Word! "The Word of God, which is the weapon of the Spirit."

Divine Measurements

We have, in former studies, been considering the eternal purpose of God in the calling of the Church. The revelation of a *mystery* through a messenger, Paul, of a ministry in the heavenlies, has held our attention, but now we are to be led into the *Divine measurements*. We look for the grand summary. We are to learn something of the higher mathematics of the spiritual world and its realities. Something of the depths of God's nature and the distances of His love!

In the first prayer, Paul prayed that we might have the "spirit of wisdom and revelation" to know three things: (1) the hope of our calling, (2) the riches of His inheritance in the saints, and (3) the exceeding greatness of His power which He wrought in Christ when He raised Him from the dead and gave Him His present seat.

The petitions of the first prayer gather about the little word "what." Three "whats": (1) "What is the hope of His calling?" (2) "What is the riches of His inheritance in the saints?" (3) "What is the exceeding greatness of His power?"

In this second prayer the petitions cluster about the word "that." The four "thats": (1) *That* He would grant you, according to the riches of His glory, to be strengthened with might by His Spirit in the inner man, (2) *That* Christ may dwell in your hearts by faith, (3) *"That"* ye being rooted and grounded in love, may be able to comprehend with all saints what is the breadth and length and depth and height, and to know the love of Christ which passeth knowledge, (4) *That* ye might be filled with all the fullness of God.

Thus we see the four "thats" in this wonderful prayer. It is a prayer for the rooting and grounding of the believer in the faith of this overwhelming revelation which God has been pleased to publish. "That ye may be able to comprehend," says the Apostle—braced up for it, "fully matched to the enterprise," says dear old John Eadie.

Then come the "measurements" and here they are: *breadth, length, depth* and *height.* Much speculation has been associated with these measurements. So much so that a church Father wisely said: "Many wits run riot in their geometrical and moral discourse upon these dimensions."

We have found more than a dozen attempts at exposition, much of it helpful, some of it entirely speculative.

Some have thought there was a reference here to the quarters of the heavens pointed to in the priestly gestures that gave name to the heave offering and the wave offering (Exod. 29:27). Some attempt to find here the mystery of the cross, as was expounded by Augustine, to signify love in its breadth, hope in its height, patience in its length and humility in its depth. Some have thought Paul here described a sphere or cube, equal in length, breadth and thickness, representing the perfection and all including infinity of God.

Erasmus saw in it God's love reaching in its heights to the

angels and in its depths into hell and stretching in its length and breadth to all the climates of the world.

Some think it is a reference to Divine wisdom. A great many commentators agree that there is reference here to the Tabernacle or the Temple, and indeed this may be the interpretation of the passage; but somehow it seems to us that we are not obliged to go outside the Epistle itself for the meaning of the passage. Indeed these dimensions or measurements appear to us to be a summary of the things previously discussed and in full harmony with the eternal purpose of God that is herein revealed. The dimensions referred to are not the dimensions of the love of Christ, for by the use of the little word "and," the love of Christ is made a separate and an additional matter.

We believe the fourfold measurements contained in this verse hold us to the main themes of the Epistle; the *Church's Redemption in Christ* and *Christ's Revelation in the Church.* Love is infinite and cannot be measured. Redemption is finite and may be measured. Redemption lies absolutely within bounds marked and measured, purposed and published by God.

Let us view the *breadth* of the eternal purpose of God as revealed in the Book of Ephesians. We have before discovered it, for we have seen the Jew and the Gentile in "one Body." Prior to the Church, Jew and Gentile were separated by a middle wall of partition between them, but the breadth of the purpose of God in the Church of God spans them both and in its breadth includes them. We are confident the Apostle is praying that with "all saints we may comprehend the breadth of God's purpose as discovered in Ephesians."

The *length* we also discovered in our former and earlier studies. We found this eternal purpose of God in the Church lying beyond and prior to the foundation of the world. The Jew was chosen from the foundation of the world, but the Church was chosen in Him before the foundation of the world.

The length to which it reaches is to the "dispensation of the fulness of times"—a distance never revealed concerning any other peoples but the members of His Body, the Church. This unquestionably is the length to which the Apostle refers in his prayer.

In the study of the measurements as to length, see 1:3 and 1:14. This is the distance covered in the Divine will and purpose in the Church.

The *depth* to which the Apostle refers is the depravity from which both Jew and Gentile were taken in the grasp of grace. In chapter 2, the early verses, this is described. While in Ephesians we scale the heights of Divine design, in chapter 2 we also look into the depths of human depravity. If you want to see the depths and the darkness of man apart from God, read Ephesians 2:1-3. This is the depth of which the apostle speaks.

The *height* is the supreme glory of this Epistle. From breadth and length and depth we now lift our eyes to the sphere which makes intelligible this entire Epistle. The height here mentioned is the "heavenlies." A sphere and location to which we are called (1:3), in which we shall be displayed (3:10), and in the hope of which we should walk worthy (4:1) and in which sphere we are now in conflict against wicked hosts (6:12). The height is the "heavenlies."

Let others speculate if they will, but we are inclined to believe that these fourfold measurements which the Apostle desires we may be "able to apprehend" are themselves the sum and substance of the Epistle and not a foreign matter introduced into this Divine and sublime argument.

Doxology

We are now bringing our study of the first half of the Epistle to the Ephesians to a close. The conclusion is the Doxology. The Apostle closed his first great sentence (1:3-14) with the words, "To the praise of His glory," and now he himself joins in the praise.

We have heard much of the purpose of God. The doxology speaks of the power of God. It is a "God who is able." The

Apostle declares that "God is able to do," "God is able to do exceeding," that "God is able to *do exceeding abundantly above* all that we ask or think," and this by the power that worketh in us, and we have learned that the power that "worketh in us" is the power that God wrought in Christ when He raised Him up and seated Him in the heavenlies (1:19, 20).

The Epistle to the Ephesians never departs from its main subject, its theme first stated continues triumphant throughout the Epistle.

How much we regret our lack of disposition for exposition! O that God will give us more grace that we may have more grasp upon these things, the breadth, and length and depth and height of which God will not be satisfied until all saints shall come to apprehend!

15

THE CONDUCT OF THE CHURCH
Ephesians 4:1-6

WE HAVE REACHED that portion of Ephesians which we define as the third division of the epistle and entitled, "The Conduct of the Church."

From the doctrine of the epistle to the deportment, we now continue the study of the Book. Following the "Amen" of the Doxology is the "I therefore" of the practical portion.

The "Calling of the Church" has been under consideration, henceforth the *conduct* and the *conflict* of the Church will claim our attention. We have been reveling in heights of heavenly revelation, we must now consider our earthly responsibility. To whom God has vouchsafed revelation there attaches great responsibility. What God has given in revelation must be continued in application.

Says the apostle Paul:

> I therefore, the prisoner of the Lord, beseech you that ye walk worthy of the vocation wherewith ye are called, with all lowliness and meekness, with longsuffering, forbearing one another in love; endeavoring to keep the unity of the Spirit in the bond of peace. There is one Body, and one Spirit, even as ye are called in one hope of your calling; one Lord, one faith, one baptism; one God and Father of all, who is above all, and through all, and in you all (Eph. 4:1-6).

Thus this "division" of the Epistle begins. There is danger in making divisions of a book of the Holy Scriptures. By such it is possible that what God has joined together, man may put asunder. Sometimes the divisions of a book are indeed the division of the book. Many times students, by seeking to set forth the order of a book, introduce disorder into the book. This should not be. There is not a commencement of something new in the Epistle to the Ephesians at this point, but there is a continuation. There is continuity and unity.

There is no change of subject, for the "heavenly calling" demands the "heavenly conduct." To turn from the doctrinal to the practical is not a break or a breach. There is no divorcement of Christian doctrine and Christian doing or between faith and works. The normal Christian walks as he talks.

The Apostle makes vital the relation between interpretation and application. A "heavenly calling" is followed by "heavenly conduct" which calls forth "heavenly conflict." There are the simple divisions of the Ephesian epistle which also argue unity. The one follows the other and we move from faith to fight.

Whatever is laid down in the doctrinal portion of this epistle is not deserted in the practical portion. Whatever follows in this portion, now under consideration, is vitally related to that which has preceded. The unity of the Book is everywhere maintained. The "vocation" results in "provocation." Let us see. The Apostle was made the chosen instrument of God to make known a "mystery" or a secret which had been "hidden." This "mystery" or secret concerned the union of Jew and Gentile in one Body—which subject we have considered together for much time and is disclosed in former chapters. Inasmuch as the Jew and the Gentile were "condemned together" and were together "dead in trespasses and sins" and were "quickened together" and "raised up together" and "seated together" and "built together" into "one Body" in Christ in the heavenlies, *then let the unity which obtains in the heavenlies be maintained in the earth.* This is the simple, yet sublime argument, and when this is understood, it will explain everything subsequently developed in this Epistle.

G. Campbell Morgan said,

> From the doctrine of the heavenly calling he passes to the duty of the earthly conduct. These, however, are not two things, they are interrelated.

On this Bishop Moule wrote:

> Scripture always brings the doctrinal into the practical, as reason and mainspring; and nowhere more than in this epistle.*

Thus we find that the unity created in the doctrinal portion of this epistle is contained in the practical; in fact, this epistle centers about "unity." Notice its threefold character:

1. The Unity Created (Eph. 2:5, 6, 14, 16, 18)

2. The Unity Continued (Eph. 4:3-6)

3. The Unity Consummated (Eph. 4:13)

In the Church, the Body of Christ, the Jew and the Gentile are one Body in the heavenlies. They must be one Body on the earth. The unity determined in the heavenlies must be displayed on the earth. We well enough know that there is only one place where the Jew and the Gentile are one, and that is in the Church. This is the one place God ever intended them to be one. In other dispensations, past and future, they are to be divided and distinct. If in the Church, the Jew and Gentile now go in one Body and are to maintain the unity of the Body, it must be accomplished as herein stated, viz., with all lowliness and meekness and long-suffering, forbearing one another in love, endeavoring to keep the unity of the Spirit in the bond of peace. There is never division, confusion or disillusion, disagreement or diversity where lowliness and meekness, long-suffering and forbearance prevail. How practical is all this, and yet how potent and with what power it comes to us in these days of divisions and dislocations! How much we should take to our hearts this exhortation! We glibly

*H. C. G. Moule, *Studies in Ephesians* (Grand Rapids: Kregel Publications, 1977), p. 103.

sing, "We are not divided, all one Body we," but in fact, there are divisions and distances between us which are not only disgusting to the world but displeasing to God. Oh, for the Divine healing of the breach in the Body of Christ! Oh, for the Divine unction to bring us to the Divine unity! Oh, that the Church of God might realize its organism rather than idealize its organizations! Says the Apostle, "There is one Body and one Spirit, even as you were called unto one hope of your calling." The hope of our calling demands the harmony of the called ones. The peace which the Blood of Christ made between the Jew and the Gentile is a bond which should not be broken. It is called by the Apostle the "bond of peace," a bond which was created by the Blood of the Redeemer. One body must of necessity have one spirit. Who could conceive of two spirits in one body with unity issuing therefrom? The telescopic unity revealed in this book is perfectly wonderful. Behold the same:

> There is one Body, and one Spirit, even as ye are called in one hope of your calling; one Lord, one faith, one baptism, one God and Father of all, who is above all, and through all, and in you all (Eph. 4:4-6).

Notice one Body, one Spirit, one calling, one Lord, one faith, one baptism, one God and Father, making a total of seven unities, which unity God has made and which unity must be kept. At what distance is the departure of the Church from this sevenfold unity we leave our readers to judge. It is a cause of much sorrow to us. But this bond of peace, which brought together Jew and Gentile into one Body, also lays the foundation for the basic unity which is to be continued and consummated in the Body. The Christian's character and conduct is not one to be lived only among the fellow members of the same Body, but it moves out into the *social sphere* in life among fellow men. It also reaches the *domestic domain*. This is as it should be, for there must be with the individual that which characterizes the incorporation.

These things will come under consideration in our next chapter.

The Spirit of God through the Apostle continues the argument by showing that the unity of the Body is declared by the diversity of the members, but "unto every one of us" says he, "is given grace according to the measure of the gift of Christ" (Eph. 4:7). This bestowal is the beneficial blessing resulting in the ascension of Christ and to some this introduction of a quotation from the Psalms appears to be out of place, but certainly it is not; for when He ascended and took His place in the heavens, it was because there was no place for Him on the earth. Having been rejected by Israel and refused by them David's throne, He sat down in the heavenlies and is now bestowing ascension blessings upon the Church. He "ascended up far above all heavens that He might fill all things" and in Ephesians 1:23 we learn that His Body is the fullness of Him that filleth all and in all. In the filling up of all things, He required the Body which is the fullness of Him that filleth all things. It would be a matter of precious profit to the student to trace through the Ephesian Epistle the continuous use of the phrase "all things." He who has purposed in the dispensation of the fullness of times to gather together in one, all things in Christ, has found Divinely necessary the Church that He might fill all things.

In the gifting and the gracing of the Church and in the diversity of bestowments, God has made contribution to its Divine unity. Paul said that, "He (God) gave some apostles; and some, prophets; and some, evangelists; and some, pastors and teachers," and this is as the revised version declares "for the perfecting of the saints unto the work of ministering unto the building up of the Body of Christ" (Eph. 4:11, 12), which diversity will ultimately issue in the unity which is Divinely desirable.

Why should we be tossed to and fro and carried about with every wind of doctrine? Why should the sleight of men who, with craftiness, bring in the wiles of error—why, we say, should these things disturb the Church of God, which is growing up in all things into Him who is the Head? Every false doctrine which divides the Church, distresses believers, disturbs harmony and peace could quickly be corrected if the calling of the Church, as revealed in the Epistle to the Ephesians, was fully understood. Proper conduct in the body of believers would properly follow the hope of such a calling as herein is revealed.

It is with sadness we must regard the failure to recognize the diversity of gifts in the unity of the Body. A young man desires to enter the ministry because he has been told that he has a good personal presence and the gift of speech. How ignoble is all this, yea, how abominable! Personal presence is nothing—the presence of God is all. Personal gifts are nothing—the gifts and graces of the Spirit are everything. God cares nothing for what we are in temperament, though He may use the same. His concern is in the truth. The human type is nothing—the Divine truth is all. It is better to trust in the Word of God than in the works of the flesh. Who has failed to notice the tendency to deprecate and depreciate the offices which God Himself has placed in the Church? Says He: "Some apostles, some prophets, some evangelists, some pastors, some teachers." Today there is a cry going up from many pastors against evangelists. Indeed there are evangelists who should be cried against, for in manner and message they are to be condemned, but the office of evangelist must not be overlooked or underrated. It is of God Himself. Those evangelists, who have been Divinely gifted and graced of God in the spirit, must be received and respected as the pastor or the teacher. They each contribute to the unity of the Body. Pastors, teachers, evangelists are all fitly joined together, compacted and companionshipped and fellowshipped "according to the effectual working in the measure of every part" (Eph. 2:16). Oh, that God may open our eyes to the holy Body and its holy unity!

Beginning at verse 17 the Apostle becomes exceedingly practical and personal. He exhorts them concerning their walk and concerning their talk. They are reminded of their past practices and their present position. They are told what to put off, what to put on and what to put away. Five times the

Apostle pertinently uses the word "let." "*Let* not the sun go down upon your wrath." "*Let* him that stole steal no more." "*Let* him labor." "*Let* no corrupt communication proceed out of your mouth." "*Let* all bitterness and wrath and clamour and evil-speaking be put away" (Eph. 4:26-32). How beautiful is the use of this word "let"! It savors not in the least of human effort to do, but speaks of the Divine power to accomplish. "Let" these things be done, *permit God to do them,* hinder not such operation, fully permit in Christian resignation, "let," child of God, He will do it, let Him do it. Those defiling sins and debasing desires thou canst not cleanse, therefore, "let." When the soul is willing God works.

16

THE BELIEVER'S SOCIAL
AND DOMESTIC LIFE
Ephesians 5:1—6:9

The Believer's Social Life (5:1-21)

THE SPIRITUAL LIFE affects the social life. Thus the Divine order is, in the present day, perverted. There is an attempt to create a social life that will create a spiritual life. This cannot be. The spiritual life will create the social life. Things set socially right cannot create things spiritually right, but when things are spiritually right they will be socially right. Without a new life in Christ there can be no true life in the community. The present day emphasis on so-called "social service" utterly ignores the spiritual life. It is of humanitarian source and knows nothing of the spiritual. The emphasis is placed upon a man's relation to his brother rather than a man's relation to his God. It is a bond of the flesh and not a bond in the faith. When man is in right relation to God, He will be in proper relation to man. Never till then.

The Epistle to the Ephesians, which is particularly a book addressed to the Church, does not deal with the subject of social service. It does not teach that the calling of the Church is to correct the social situation, it distinctly declares the days to be "evil" and exhorts that they be "redeemed" (5:16). It does not deal with the solidarity of society, but with the union of believers. It is not a question of community of society but the communion of saints. It is not social service which is urged, but sacrificial service. It is as children to God, created so in Christ Jesus, that the Apostle Paul is here exhorting. We are delivered from the former hate. We have put on the "new man" and put off the "old man," therefore the "lets" of the concluding portion of chapter 4. Now we are to walk in love and in light. Filthiness and foolishness are gone. There is no departure here from the exhortation concerning the maintaining of unity. Having had our "old man crucified" with Him, we are now united to the new. Our identification with Christ was not at the incarnation, but rather in His resurrection. Between the old life and the new life there are a number of sharply and spiritually drawn contrasts. Formerly it was falsehood, now it is *truth;* formerly malice, now *mercy;* formerly stealing, now *giving;* formerly corrupt speech, now *edifying speech.* It was formerly hatred, hereafter it is *love.* The past life was filled with impurity, hereafter *purity;* formerly there was folly and foolishness, now *faithfulness,* but the dynamic for it all is the Divine calling and the power for the accomplishment is the power which God wrought in Christ, that the believer might enjoy the position he has in Christ. "God is love," "walk in love" (5:1, 2). "God is light," "walk as children of light" (5:8). If God is light, fellowship with Him and "have no fellowship with the unfruitful works of darkness" (5:11). "God is light," therefore walk as in the light (5:13). Arise from the darkness of death, and "Christ shall give thee light" (5:14). Be not filled with spirits producing drunkenness, "but be filled with the Holy Spirit" (5:18). Indeed this entire portion is a book of instruction for the *walk of the believer.* There is *not a social evil that is not rebuked,* nor a *spiritual need that is not supplied,* and every exhortation is to be obeyed in the light of the opening exhortation at 4:1, "Walk worthy."

The Believer's Domestic Life (5:22—6:9)

Not only do we behold the social sphere, but we move also into the innermost domain of the domestic. The Apostle intrudes the Christian faith into the family. Here unity also is to prevail and to be preserved. The husband, as Christ, is at the head, the wife, as the Church, is subject to the head. The divorcement of this Divine order is the cause of the disorder and disruption in multitudes of homes. The minister of God who is called upon to officiate at the solemn marriage ceremony is often exhorted by the bride, to be sure to "leave out the word 'obey.' " But God has not left out the word obey. Any woman who is not ready to obey the man she marries is not in proper relation and has not sufficient love for the man who seeks to marry her. "Christ loved the Church and gave Himself for the Church" (Eph. 6:25). The husband loves the wife and is to give himself for the wife. Where love is supreme, obedience may be complete. The married life of Spirit-filled believers takes on the mystical meaning which exists between Christ and the Church. All that the Church is to Christ, the wife is to be to the husband. All that Christ is to the Church, the husband is to the wife. Thus the unity is marvelously marked. Paul declares this is a "great mystery," but marriage in which this mystery with its deep meaning is not understood or is misunderstood is a marriage of meaninglessness. As Christ and the Church are united, so also the husband and the wife. They are members one of another as believers are members of His Body.

Children are next brought into view (Eph. 6:1-4). The unity is also maintained, for children are the product of union of husband and wife, also fathers as the heads of the house are exhorted to maintain proper relation to their offspring. The Ephesian Epistle knows nothing of present day practice of fathers delegating to the mother the care and conduct of the children. The father must hold his place of headship over the children as well as the wife. Fathers must not provoke their "children to anger," and children are to be "nurtured."

The average parents today know nothing of this "nurture," but few children are "nurtured." This superficial and artificial age has changed the word "nurture" to "culture." They want their children cultured, not nurtured, therefore they seek to culture their children and fail to nurture them and what a thankless brood they have! It is but little wonder that Paul, in describing to Timothy conditions prevailing in the latter times, said, "Disobedience to parents." Ephesians says, "Obedience, children," "nurture, fathers," but the fathers nurture not, and the children obey not, and this sad situation could be corrected by the instruction of the Epistle to the Ephesians. Parents see that their children get *education* at any price, but nothing for their *edification* is provided. Yes, education has taken the place of edification and culture the place of nurture. We have heard parents say, "My child must learn to dance to be graceful." They desire grace for her person, forgetting that her greatest need is grace in the heart. The failure of fathers in the instruction and correction of their children is startlingly exemplified in the Holy Scriptures. How severely God smote Eli for his failure to constrain and restrain his sons! The bitterest cup David ever drank was the wickedness of Absalom and Adonijah. In the latter's case we learned the secret: "And his father had not displeased him at any time in saying, 'Why hast thou done so'?" (1 Kings 1:6). Children cannot grow up without righteous rebuke. Does any son love his father because, over his father's authority, he always gets his own way? Certainly not. Adonijah rose up against him and pushed him off his throne. All that read will agree that the Book of Ephesians holds instruction which is greatly needed in the domestic circles of the present time. Husbands, wives, children, read and study Ephesians 5:21—6:4.

Then there is the problem of the servant in the house. It is a question of social equality and inequality. It is the problem of social distinction and differences, but even here unity must prevail. With God there is no respect of persons (Eph. 6:9). The place one may fill does not depreciate the person they are. Servants are exhorted to obedience, knowing that their service is unto Christ.

G. Campbell Morgan has said, with much meaning, "As to servants, the key for their service is that it is to be unto Christ." As to masters, the pattern of their authority is given in the declaration, "your master is Christ," therefore we find the master and the servant. When the servant serves in the sight of Christ and the master subjects in the light of Christ, there is Divine unity preserved. How practical is all this portion of Ephesians and yet how powerful! How simple and yet how spiritual, how human and yet how Divine!

17

THE CONFLICT OF THE CHURCH
Ephesians 6:10-18

WE HAVE BEEN throughout Ephesians tracing a new word of Scripture which we found at the very opening of the Epistle— the word "heavenly" (Eph. 1:3). We have studied the heavenly calling of the Church, the heavenly conduct of the Church, and now the heavenly conflict of the Church.

The apostle Paul said:

> Put on the whole armour of God, that ye may be able to stand against the wiles of the devil. For we wrestle not against flesh and blood, but against principalities, against powers, against the rulers of the darkness of this world, against spiritual wickedness in high places (Eph. 6:11, 12).

Here we find the conflict of the Church to be in the same sphere and locality as the calling of the Church, viz.: "heavenly places" or the "heavenlies." This is in harmony with the trend of the Epistle and altogether to be expected at the end of the Epistle. If the Church is called into the "heavenlies" and is to exercise a future ministry in the "heavenlies," then the present conflict of the Church is waged against it from the "heavenlies."

There is a present "wrestle," a warfare waged—but not against flesh and blood—members of the Church, the Body of Christ have been delivered from a flesh and blood bond,— therefore no occasion to wrestle against flesh and blood. The Church is not contending for a position and place on the earth where "flesh and blood" is in contest, and conflict for a possession, therefore the conflict must come from another sphere and from enemies of a different character and kind.

Flesh and blood of the three great divisions of mankind are today in conflict—they contend for the earth. The nations struggle against nations. The Church is neither Jew nor Gentile, bond nor free, therefore has no part or place in the struggle. Indeed speaking strictly within the Scriptures, the Church is not even on the earth, it is viewed by God as seated with Christ in the heavenlies. Positionally it is there, conditionally it is here, but spiritually it must reckon itself dead, buried, raised and seated with Christ in heavenly places. If the conflict of the Church is not against "flesh and blood," against who is it?

"Against principalities, against powers, against the rulers of the darkness of the world, against spiritual wickedness in heavenly places" (Eph. 6:12).

Four times "against." Four "things" against: "principalities," "powers," "rulers of darkness," and "spiritual wickedness."

The Enemy (6:11-12)

Let us ponder and consider these persons and powers of the underworld now holding possession and position in the upper world. Who are they? Where are they? Why are they?

They are wicked spiritual hosts in military organization camped and entrenched in the heavenlies. They are invisible agents of wickedness in an organized spirit world. They are the rulers of the darkness of this age. They actually exercise rule over this world in this age time of darkness and delusion. They direct the energy of the age. They are unquestionably organized in military order. Militarism not only prevails on the earth but maintains in the heavenlies. Intimations and allusions to this organization may be found in Ephesians 1:21, Colossians 2:15. The Book of Revelation seems to open into this very sphere and describes a future struggle. See Rev. 12:7-9. The leaders of these hosts alone are mentioned.

When Christ was raised up from the dead and exalted to the highest point in the universe, He passed through these organized ranks, who were powerless to prevent Him passing through and up. Says Ephesians 1:21: "Far above all *principality,* and *power,* and *might,* and *dominion.*" Christ has been raised infinitely above them and they wait beneath His feet for their future humiliation and casting down.

From Gethsemane to the glory, Christ was engaged in mighty conflict. In the Garden, Satan attempted to send Him to the cross bereft of His reason or to kill Him before He reached the cross and thus refute the Divine plan and purpose in redemption by the Blood of His cross. In this he failed. At the cross the serpent met the "woman's seed" and scored a seeming victory. He bruised the heel of the "woman's seed," beyond the heel he had no power and the heel he bruised will in turn bruise his head and this shortly. Read Romans 16:20. The cross was Satan's defeat. Here God's David takes the sword of Goliath and pierces him with a mortal wound.

Satan's attempt to hold Him in the grave, that He might see corruption, also failed. It was not possible for "death to hold Him" and He saw "no corruption." If He had been born of Adam's nature He would have come to the end of Adam's progeny, but He was declared "the Son of God . . . by the resurrection from the dead" (Rom. 1:4). He arose from the dead! He was the first fruits of them that sleep. "They that are Christ's at His coming" (2 Cor. 15:23). (Come quickly Lord Jesus!) The law took Him to the grave but had no power to keep Him in the grave.

Again, however, Christ must meet the enemy—this time at the ascension and enthronement. Satan had delighted in His humiliation not knowing that it was the basis and ground of His exaltation. We read in Philippians 2:8, 9, "The death of the cross, *wherefore* God also hath highly exalted Him." The cross is the instrument of His exaltation. The route to His exaltation is by way of ascension: "He has gone into heaven," says Peter, "and is on the right hand of God; angels and authorities and powers being made subject unto Him" (1 Pet.

3:22). They did not become subject unto Him without struggle. Not willingly, for Peter is not speaking of unfallen angels, for they remained subject to Him, but of fallen and rebellious angels and spirits who are made subject unto Him. They opposed His ascent. Having failed to keep Him from the cross they now unite in an attempt to defeat Him from reaching the throne. For they know that once upon the throne it will be but a short time until His enemies are His "footstool" (Ps. 110:1). He is to sit upon His Father's throne only "until." He awaits an advent. His ascent assures His advent. *His position* now above them and *His purpose* to return to the earth will result in their being cast down. He will sweep them before Him and rout them from their position.

In our judgment the great conflict of Christ was not only through His earthly life, in the Garden of Gethsemane, Gabatha, Golgotha, the grave; but it extended into the heavenlies at the ascension, where He met with a hate and hostility exceeding anything previously experienced. The twenty-fourth Psalm may speak of this event and ascent. "Let the King of Glory come in," cries the voice of a watcher within the gate. Who is the Lord? "The Lord strong and mighty, the Lord mighty in battle" (Ps. 24:8), is the answer. What battle? The Battle of Gethsemane! The Battle of Calvary! The Battle of Joseph's Tomb! The Battle of the Ascent! Let Him in! It is the Mighty God-Man Warrior!

There was opposition to His ascension: there was attempt at prevention. With the might and majesty which character- ized every movement of His redemptive program, He passed through "principalities, powers, might and dominion." He went "far above" them. They are far beneath His feet rather than above His head.

Having failed to defeat Christ, the Head of the Church, they now turn their attention to the Church, the Body of Christ. God has purposed that the "heavenlies" will be the sphere of the future service of the Church (see Eph. 3:10). Its calling is *heavenly,* its ministry will be *heavenly,* therefore its conflict is *"heavenly."* The place now occupied by "wicked hosts" will be then occupied by the Church. The Church must realize the character of this conflict and be properly armored. "Put on the whole armour of God," says the Apostle, "that ye may be able to stand against the wiles of the devil." The word wile is "stratagem," cunning art of a spiritual foe. Not a flesh and blood conflict where human wit must meet human wit, but a warfare issuing for the secret counsels of a world of darkness and demons. This is the one and only sphere of the conflict and contest of the Church. All other enmity to the Church is created and promoted from this seat of antagonism.

Satan seeks to blind the eyes of believers to their heavenly calling and heavenly conflict. His purpose is to keep the hope of the Church centered upon the earth. Today we hear much in great public meetings of what the Church has lost. Some say, "The Church has lost its power." Others say, "The Church has lost its vision, the Church has lost reverence, passion," and what not? The real loss of the Church is its primitive calling,—*its early hope.* With the return of this hope of the calling all else will be returned and restored. The Epistle to the Ephesians is what the Church needs. A vast majority of its ministers are in utter ignorance of this "calling" and this "conflict." To some we write as fools. A multitude of ministers admonish the Church to a world task. The Church is bent to this hopeless task when it should be erect and alert to this heavenly hope.

For our part we do not urge the Church into the work of reformation but unto the hope of translation. We do not exhort the Church to seek a home on the earth but to hold a hope in the heavenlies. We believe God's purpose and plan is better than the propaganda of man. Though often severely criticized we can hold no other hope in the light of a rightly divided Word.

The Weapons (6:13-17)

The only weapons of warfare necessary for the Church or any member of it will be found in this passage (Eph. 6:13-17). They alone are sufficient to meet the enemy against which we wrestle. Here are the weapons: *Truth, righteousness,* the *Gospel of peace, faith* and the *Word of God.* With these only can the Church stand against the wiles of the wicked one. This panoply is sufficient for the persons and powers against us. *Let us fight in the armor of the Lord.* Let us lay aside human mailed fists and suits of armor. The whole armor of God is enough for the Church of God. The day is evil. Let us stand in the only armor in which we can stand against such foes.

Truth which is ours by Divine revelation, *Righteousness* which is ours by Divine imputation, *Peace* which is ours by Divine reconciliation, *Faith* which is ours by Divine impartation and the *Word of God* which is ours by the Spirit's interpretation, is enough to fully equip the Church for its warfare!

18

RESOURCE FOR VICTORY
Ephesians 6:18-20

BEING FULLY EQUIPPED as above for victorious warfare, the Christian Church and all the individual warriors have unlimited resource (prayer) to sustain themselves and their fellow saints (v. 18).

The apostle Paul asked his readers to remember him in intercessory prayer because he himself was up against the attacks of the enemy (6:18-20). Particularly he asked that "I may open my mouth boldly, to make known the mystery of the gospel" (v. 19) that he had mentioned previously (Eph. 3:3-6). He does not request prayer for his physical freedom from the chains of imprisonment, having been a "prisoner of Jesus Christ" (3:1 and 4:1). His main concern was that he might take the most advantage of his circumstances and, as an "Ambassador in bonds," i.e., in chains, he would be outspoken in testimony to others. A strange situation: instead of receiving a dignified and respected treatment that a representative of a foreign government should receive, Paul, representing the Lord Jesus Christ, is tied by chains. A brief look at Acts 28:20 will convince us of the fact that his prayer was answered during his imprisonment.

PART 5
CONCLUSION
Ephesians 6:21-24

CONCLUSION
Ephesians 6:21-24

THE APOSTLE desires to comfort the hearts of his friends at Ephesus by having Tychicus (v. 21) report personally to them, as he did to the Colossian church (Col. 4:7, 8), and thus give them more detailed reports of what actually was happening to their spiritual father.

Paul's closing remarks include a triple benediction of peace, love with faith, and grace (vv. 23, 24). The first "peace" was the common form of salutation in the East but also speaks of the spiritual blessings which result from reconciliation with God through Jesus Christ.

The second blessing is that of "love" that accompanies true faith because it is the fruit of faith. Paul had a faithful love toward his brethren inspite of the difficult circumstances through which he had come. No doubt he also had in mind the love of God which never changes.

And finally "grace" is extended to all those who respond with faithfulness and love to the love of God. To "love our Lord Jesus Christ in sincerity" is to love with incorruptness, i.e., "with a pure heart; without dissembling; without hypocrisy."*

---

*Albert Barnes, *Barnes' Notes on the New Testament* (Grand Rapids: Kregel Publications, 1962), p. 1016.

BOOKS BY W. LEON TUCKER

STUDIES IN ROMANS

Proper interpretation is the foundation for this valuable treatise on the Epistle to the Romans. The main doctrinal themes—condemnation, justification, sanctification and glorification—are clearly examined. The author offers much insight into the importance of the parenthetical portion (Romans 9—11) of this Pauline Epistle.

Unique seed thoughts for sermon preparation are scattered throughout this *Studies in Romans*. This book is especially helpful to get a good panoramic view of this important Epistle.

STUDIES IN EPHESIANS

This portion-by-portion commentary is true to the text and spiritually rich. The author uses careful exegesis as the basis for this unique work with instruction for believer's oneness in Christ. Well-researched facts are given, and many key outlines and alliterations are offered making this a practical study-guide for the Bible student interested in the calling, the conduct, and the conflict of the church.

STUDIES IN REVELATION

Tucker's expository commentary is of superb structure. Written in a simple, direct style, its prophetic truths are easily grasped. A pastor will find this well-outlined book an excellent guide to lead his flock through a study of the Book of Revelation. This volume will also accommodate the Christian teacher who desires an excellent textbook for a class study. The practical helps and suggestions make this volume a veritable gold mine for those desiring truths for practical living or preaching.